LEGEND

INGRID BERGMAN

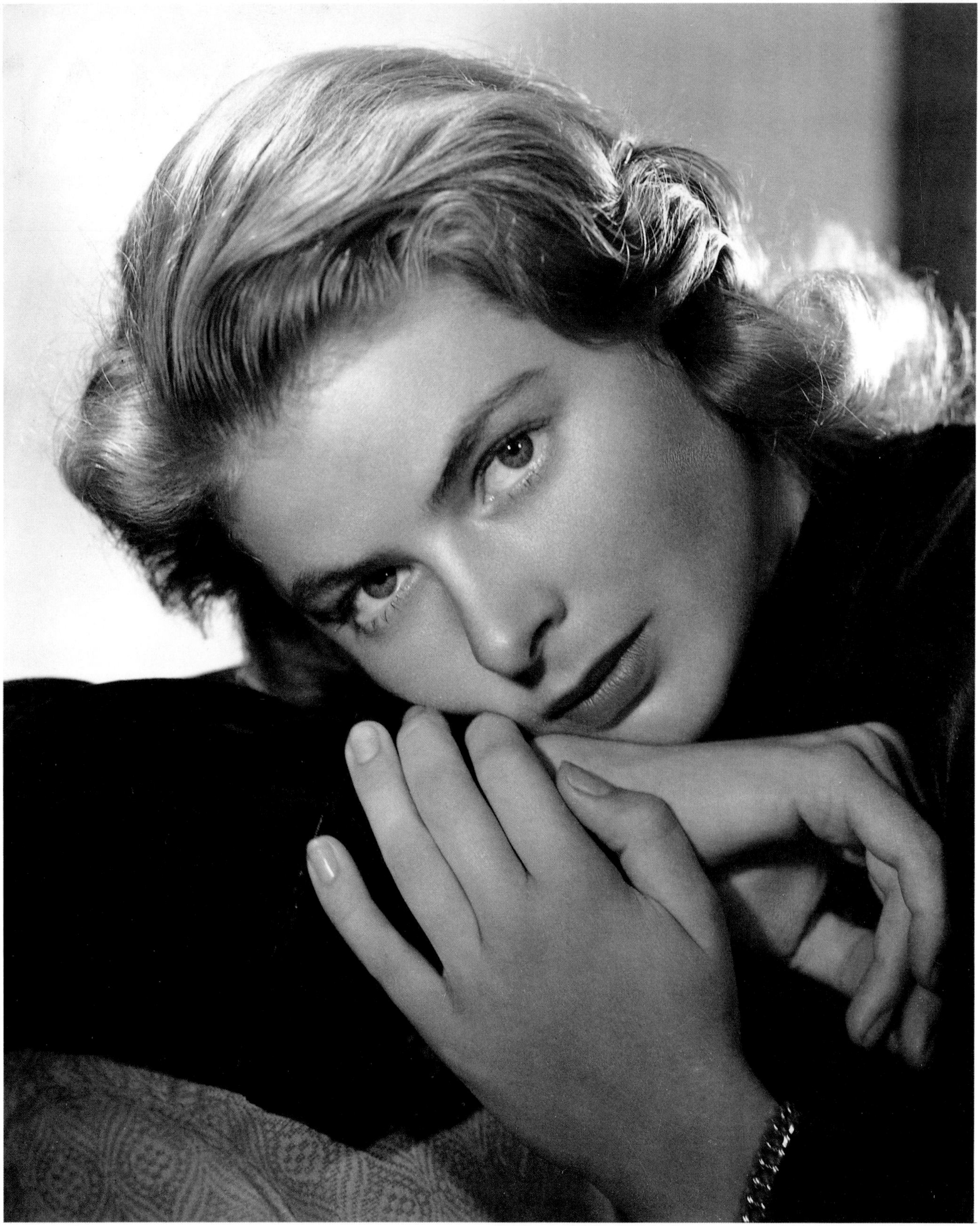

INGRID BERGMAN

INTRODUCTION BY SHERIDAN MORLEY

SERIES EDITOR JOHN KOBAL

Photographs from
THE KOBAL COLLECTION

PAVILION
MICHAEL JOSEPH

First published in Great Britain in 1985 by
Pavilion Books Limited
196 Shaftesbury Avenue, London WC2H 8JL
in association with Michael Joseph Limited
44 Bedford Square, London WC1B 3DP

Introduction © 1985 Sheridan Morley

Afterword © 1985 John Kobal

Photographs © 1985 The Kobal Collection

Designed by Craig Dodd

All rights reserved. No part of this publication
may be reproduced, stored in a retrieval system,
or transmitted, in any form or by any means electronic,
mechanical, photocopying, recording or otherwise
without prior permission of the copyright holder.

British Library Cataloguing in Publication Data
   Ingrid Bergman.—(Legends)
   1. Bergman, Ingrid, *1915–1982*   2. Moving-pictures
   actors and actresses—United States—
   Biography
   I. Series
   791.43'028'0924   PN2287.8435

ISBN 0–907516–90–4

Printed and bound in Japan by Dai Nippon

CONTENTS

INGRID BERGMAN
by Sheridan Morley

THE PHOTOGRAPHS

PHOTOGRAPHY
FILM STARS AND ART
by John Kobal

List of Photographs

1

YR-40

INGRID BERGMAN

When, after a brave seven-year battle against cancer, Ingrid Bergman died at her home in London on her sixty-seventh birthday in August 1982, television stations around the world reached for *Casablanca*. Forty years on, everybody was still going to Rick's. That was what it had originally been called: *Everybody Goes To Rick's*. Just another unsuccessful Broadway drama that was to become a legendary Hollywood movie: 'Play it once, Sam, for old time's sake. Play it, Sam. Play *As Time Goes By*'. 'I remember every detail. The Germans wore grey; you wore blue'. 'If you're not with him when that plane leaves the ground you'll regret it. Maybe not today, maybe not tomorrow, but soon and for the rest of your life . . . I'm no good at being noble, but it doesn't take much to see that the problems of three little people don't amount to a hill o'beans in this crazy world. . . . Here's looking at you, kid'.

But why? Why, looking back over a career that spanned half a century and three Academy Awards and very nearly fifty films, and earned four million dollars do we instinctively think back to Rick's? Talking to Ingrid late one night at a theatre restaurant in Chichester, where she was celebrating her sixtieth year with a revival of *Waters of the Moon*, I discovered that she had no idea either:

'Maybe because it keeps turning up on television and in retrospectives. They have a film society at Harvard where it's shown every year, and one time the soundtrack broke down and two students sat on the stage and spoke all the dialogue in time with our lip movements. That's how well they knew it. But I hardly knew Bogart then, and he was such a shy man that at night after the shooting I used to creep downtown and watch all his old movies in Los Angeles cinemas, hoping that way I'd find out something more about the kind of man he was. Neither of us knew how the movie was supposed to end: they wrote two versions, in one of which I went off in the plane with Paul Henreid and in the other I stayed on the ground with Bogart. Either way I think it would have worked: it was that kind of a film.'

Bergman was one of the very few actresses who ever brought true distinction to Hollywood, and like Katharine Hepburn she achieved that by the constant suggestion that there was a world elsewhere. For Ingrid of course there was, though not always a very safe or easy one: when she died, I happened to be in Hollywood and as that film community went into instant videotape mourning with screenings of her early films, I couldn't help remembering that this was the same nervous and hypocritical community which had shamefully exiled her thirty years earlier for carrying an illegitimate child and (perhaps worse) abandoning the California studios to live and work on location in Italy with the child's father Roberto Rossellini.

At the time, she had just made the Maxwell Anderson *Joan of Arc* and my father happened to be with her at one screening, not an easy occasion, since the film had already been picketed by the League of American Mothers who were soon to threaten to have her as-yet unborn Rossellini child forcibly adopted to spare it the supposed 'shame' of an Italian life. As she left the screening, which was understandably less than triumphant, Bergman turned to Robert and said simply 'Perhaps I should have done the Bernard Shaw version instead'.

By the time I got to know her in the 1960s, it was as a stage actress; all but one of her major films were long past, and she was making periodic royal tours of the West End in a succession of heavily upholstered semi-classic revivals. Sometimes, though, she would suddenly start talking about the past, about Bogie, about that haunting romantic uncertainty of *Casablanca*, or about Jean Renoir who had refused to work with her when both were at the height of their Hollywood fame but who promised that if ever she became a falling star he would catch her and restore her to fortune, something he then achieved in 1956 with the lyrical *Elena*.

But in the end, Bergman was her own greatest invention and protection. Like Chaplin, she survived years of Hollywood blacklisting by the simple expedient of proving that films needed her more than she needed them. Like Garbo, another graduate of the Royal Stockholm Theatre School, Bergman managed never to get totally remodelled by the dream factory, and like nobody else on earth or screen she made you believe that Rick's Cafe really was in Casablanca instead of the back lot at Warner's, and that the

3

earth really was moving in *For Whom The Bell Tolls*, for neither of which films, incidentally, was she Hollywood's first choice.

But when she talked about that extraordinary professional and private past, about the early film triumphs and the great Rossellini romance and the more sedate European years which followed it, already that past seemed to belong to someone completely different. The ice queen had somehow become the earth mother, and of all the gin joints in all the world we were extremely lucky that she walked into ours. For the courage with which Bergman lived that remarkable life, and the even greater courage with which she faced up to a long and painful death, they ought to have inscribed on her memorial the single word 'Undaunted'.

Just a year after she died, the Italian Red Cross for which she had worked in her Rossellini years arranged an unforgettable week-long tribute to Bergman: the wife of President Fanfani organised a gathering in Venice of Gregory Peck, Charlton Heston, Olivia de Havilland, Claudette Colbert, Audrey Hepburn, Walter Matthau, Liza Minnelli, Ann Todd, Roger Moore, and Dudley Moore, together with various husbands, wives, children and retainers. This nostalgia starfest was essentially a fund-raising event in Ingrid's honour, and though Casablanca may be some way from the lagoons of Venice, we could at least reflect that the Hemingway of *For Whom the Bell Tolls* was just another hack from Harry's Bar.

The Italians have constructed entire opera houses on more tenuous connections, and when two thousand of us gathered in La Fenice to watch some Bergman home movies, it was an evening of rare delight. When she was about three years old, Ingrid's parents acquired what must have been one of the first movie cameras in Stockholm and from then until their death when she was still very young, they recorded her earliest public appearances in parks, playgrounds, back gardens and the streets of the city. This fragmentary, flickery, hugely evocative footage dating from about 1920 and now wonderfully edited by Ingmar Bergman (a friend, no relation) runs no more than twenty minutes but deserves a vastly wider showing.

4

Watching it at the Fenice that August night, and listening to the speeches that were made about Bergman afterwards by leaders of the local film industry, I suddenly realised that perceptions of Ingrid depend entirely on which country you happen to be in at the time. In Sweden, as is their chauvinist custom, they never forgave her (and indeed in later years barracked one of her rare stage appearances) for going off to Hollywood; in Hollywood they never forgave her for going off to Rossellini; but in Italy none of that matters at all. The Italians' Ingrid Bergman isn't our Ingrid at all: not for them, that night, any mention of *Casablanca* or Bogart or Rick's Café or playing it again, Sam; not for them the Bergman of *Gaslight* or *Spellbound* or *Anastasia*, the Bergman who abandoned stardom and propriety to run off with some lousy unknown foreign director and have his illegitimate child.

Where for years the American and even the British press regarded Bergman's Rossellini years, the years of *Stromboli* and *Europa*, as an unfortunate romantic and artistic aberration in an otherwise glowing commercial career, the Italians (and perhaps rightly?) seem to regard them as her years of true film distinction. Now that Rossellini is at last being upwardly revalued by film schools everywhere, the Bergman career may also have to be seen in an altogether new light.

It is not as though she had ever intended to be a Hollywood movie star: the only surviving child of an unsuccessful painter-turned-photographer and a mother who died when Ingrid was three, she was brought up in Stockholm by a bevy of aunts, all deeply disapproving of her father's subsequent affair with a governess half his age whom he had first hired to look after his little daughter. But her father died when Ingrid was only twelve, and one of the aunts had a heart attack and followed him only six months later. Bergman entered her teens without close relatives, brought up among cousins with whom she had little in common, and therefore inclined as soon as possible to escape into a never-never land of school plays.

At seventeen, against considerable opposition from uncles and aunts who told her not unfairly that she was awkward and ungainly and would do better perhaps as a

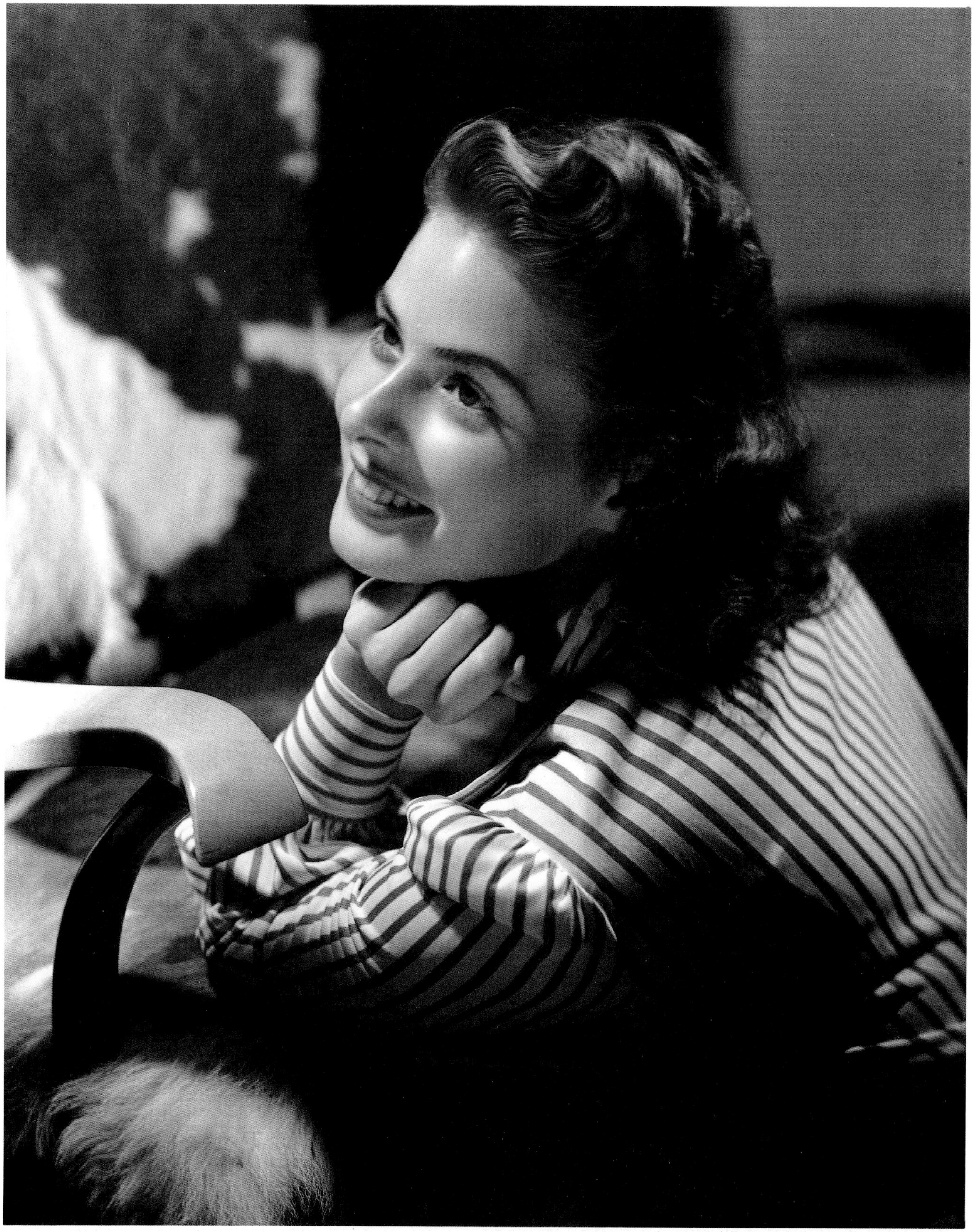

secretary, Ingrid got into the Royal Theatre School where one of the most enthusiastic judges at her audition for entry was prophetically not a stage but a film director, the great Alf Sjoberg. A year or so later, well before her twentieth birthday, it was another film director Gustav Molander (the brother of the school's principal) who put her in front of a studio camera for the very first time. The film was *Munkbrogreven* (1934) and Ingrid was cast as the maid of a run-down hotel supplying illegal liquor to young bohemians. Critics found her 'hefty', and indeed stills of the period do show a rather podgy full-cheeked blonde, the kind of Mädchen you might have expected to find playing the innkeeper's lovelorn daughter in a minor Viennese operetta of the period.

A formidable row then broke out between the Molander brothers: Olof, who ran the theatre school, argued that Ingrid's had not been an especially impressive screen debut, and that she should at once return to complete the three-year stage course at his school before going into the theatre as originally planned. Gustav on the other hand argued that he had found a natural screen talent, and that she should leave school at once and sign a contract with him for at least three years. In return, he would pay her a minimum of five thousand kronor a year, and allow her time off from filming for occasional stage appearances as well as continued training in voice and movement.

Unsurprisingly she chose the movie contract, and was rewarded with an immediate starring role in *Branningar* (1935) where she was cast as a fisherman's daughter bearing the illegitimate child of a local Lutheran priest who then conveniently gets struck by lightning and cannot remember what he has done, at least until the last reel when it all comes back to him and he abandons his ministry to become a farmer with Ingrid and the baby happily at his side. Surprisingly, this too did well at the box-office and Molander now decided that he would take personal charge of Ingrid's career, directing in all more than half of the ten pre-Hollywood films she was to make in Sweden and Germany.

This of course was the era of great director-female star partnerships (von Sternberg with Dietrich, Paul Czinner with Bergner) and it may well have been that, like those other European directors, Molander saw in his new star a passport to Hollywood for them both. For now however, feeling that he might have pushed her too far too fast towards stardom, Molander cast Ingrid as the second female lead in two more melodramas, *Swedenhielms* and *Valborgsmassoafton* (both 1935), in the latter of which she was seen as the daughter of Sweden's greatest actor/director Victor Seastrom and the secretary of Garbo's former co-star Lars Hanson. If her roles had got smaller, the professional company she was keeping was now of Sweden's best. Then, deciding perhaps that enough talent and screen education might now have rubbed off on her, Molander gave her another crack at solo female stardom in *Pa Solsidan* (1936) where she played an orphaned bank clerk torn between the love of a young writer and that of an older and richer landowner. This was the first of Bergman's films to get an (albeit very restricted) American showing in one or two of New York's foreign-language cinemas, but it was seen there by a diligent *Variety* critic who noted that Bergman was 'pretty and capable, rating a Hollywood berth'. By the look of the stills, she had already lost several pounds and a tendency to pull funny faces at the camera.

It was at this time that Ingrid, still only twenty-one, ceased to regard Molander as her sole guide and mentor. She had met a Swedish dentist nearly ten years her senior, Petter Lindstrom, whose steady influence on her life and career seemed to provide the security she had never enjoyed as a fatherless teenager; they were married in July 1937, and were still married a decade later when Bergman wrote her famous request for work to Rossellini.

Lindstrom and Molander proved a formidable private and professional partnership in guiding Bergman's life over the next decade: in 1937 Molander himself wrote and then directed a screenplay about a young pianist falling in love with an older and married violinist. The film was of course the first *Intermezzo*, with Gosta Ekman as the tortured musician and Bergman in one of those rare, magical performances where you can actually watch a great star being born in the confines of less than ninety minutes. The film made her Sweden's top box-office attraction of 1937, and two years later the Selznick remake was to make her Hollywood career: but for now there was no sign of

American interest, and Bergman at last took advantage of the clause in her film contract which said that she could from time to time have leave to work in the theatre.

She therefore made her stage debut in Stockholm in a couple of minor comedies, both of which thrived on the success of *Intermezzo* which was playing at neighbouring cinemas but neither of which convinced either Bergman or her director (Molander, also making a rare theatrical detour) that her true home was anywhere other than a film studio. Soon therefore she was back in front of the cameras in yet another mindless comedy called *Dollar*, but Ingrid, backed now by intelligent advice and support from Lindstrom, knew that she needed a drama to keep her career on the winning streak that had started with *Intermezzo*. The one she found was *En Evinnas Ansikte*, the story of a woman with a disfigured face who achieves a whole new life and personality after an operation: as *A Woman's Face*, this was later to give Joan Crawford one of her most successful and archetypal Hollywood roles but for now Bergman had to convince an unwilling Swedish studio to give it a try, something they eventually only agreed to do if Ingrid in turn would agree to star in yet another bland social romance, this one (*Only One Night*, 1938) concerned with a poor little rich girl falling for a circus artist.

By now there was worldwide interest in Bergman's screen future: in New York, David O Selznick's assistant Kay Brown had already seen the Swedish *Intermezzo* and was beginning to suggest that David might have here the next great European import for Hollywood. Slightly quicker off the mark were the UFA studios in Berlin: Bergman's mother had been German and Ingrid already spoke the langauge, so UFA now offered a three-picture deal to start with *Die Vier Gesellen* (*The Four Companions*). Though she was already carrying Pia, her only Lindstrom child and the girl who was to grow up into one of the most beautiful and successful New York television reporters of the 1980s, and though the war was barely a year away, neither Ingrid nor Petter saw any reason not to take up the UFA deal, at least at the outset. She made the first film, was taken by the director to a Hitler rally which she didn't care for, and only after the shooting was completed, driving around the rest of Europe in the summer of 1938, did the Lindstroms begin to think that perhaps the remainder of her contract with the Nazi-controlled UFA organisation should now be reconsidered in the light of what was almost certainly going to be a World War.

Besides, there was now an altogether more attractive foreign deal in the offing: on 16 August 1938, having seen *Intermezzo*, Selznick wired Kay Brown in New York with instructions to a) find out whether Bergman was indeed the girl he'd liked so much in that film since he had found the Swedish credit titles somewhat confusing, and b) if so, to get her a course of English lessons and a boat ticket to New York. By October he had had second thoughts: maybe it would seem more sensible just to buy the script of *Intermezzo* and remake it in English with Loretta Young and Charles Boyer? By February 1939 his instructions to Kay Brown were that Miss Bergman should indeed be bought and brought from Sweden, but maybe under a different name and certainly not with a massive publicity build-up since 'foreign importations have reached a point where the American public resents overseas players unless they sneak in like Hedy Lamarr'. By Spring 1939 however, Bergman had duly arrived in Hollywood and Selznick (already dealing with one much-publicized foreign female film star as Vivien Leigh completed *Gone With The Wind* for him) was in a state of high panic: 'I note' he wired Miss Brown on 18 March, 'that Bergman is 69½ inches tall. Is it possible she is actually this high, and if so will we have to use stepladders with Leslie Howard?'

The original offer from Selznick via Kay Brown to Bergman had been the ritual seven-year contract with rather more options on his side than hers: it did however guarantee that her first film in Hollywood would be the remake of *Intermezzo*, and that meant she would be starting from a position of strength denied to any other of the European stars who had gone west in search of greater film fame. Even so, she was undecided: in the winter of 1938, with Pia only a few months old and a Swedish film industry eager to welcome her home from Berlin, California seemed a very long way away. Suppose the war did come, and she were cut off there from her new family in Stockholm? Suppose *Intermezzo* was a disaster in English?

In long discussions with both Lindstroms at their home in Stockholm, Kay Brown reached a compromise that seemed to suit even Selznick: Ingrid would not sign his seven-year contract, but she would sign for *Intermezzo* and give him an option on one further film if it worked out well enough. That kept all her other professional, domestic and geographic options wide open, which at the beginning of 1939 was surely not a bad idea. Accordingly Ingrid went out alone to California for the three months that it would take to shoot the new *Intermezzo*, and Selznick graciously agreed that she might as well keep her own name since 'Ingrid Lindstrom' was 'just as forgettable' and he hadn't got any other ideas. He was, however, appalled by her problems with the English language, and by the fact that some of her rushes seemed to him to display 'a complete lack of beauty'. In a memo of 9 June 1939 to his lighting cameraman Selznick noted sharply 'that curious charm she had in the Swedish version of *Intermezzo*, the combination of exciting beauty and fresh purity, certainly ought to be within our abilities to capture. It would be shocking indeed if some cameraman in a small Stockholm studio was proven to be able to do so much superior work with her than we are.'

Then again, there was the height problem: Selznick thought she still looked 'titanic' next to Leslie Howard, and worried that publicists were already comparing her to such other and more exotic foreign imports as Garbo and Dietrich 'with whom she cannot possibly compete'. He wasn't even sure they had got the title right: advisers thought that *Love Story* or *Memory of Love* or even *Sacred and Profane Love* might look better at the box-office than the somewhat highbrow *Intermezzo*, and eventually it was decided to add either 'A Love Story' or 'Escape to Happiness' as a kind of reassuring subtitle for the unmusical. The filming was not exactly easy, especially as Selznick quarrelled with the director William Wyler on the first day of shooting and replaced with him Gregory Ratoff, but Selznick was much taken with Bergman's health-and-efficiency look of the great outdoors, one that he saw as a welcome contrast to the sophistication of her

6

rivals: Vivien Leigh was indeed told at this time by David, and to her fury, that she was wearing far too much make-up and should emulate 'the Bergman look'.

But the deal was still for this one film only, and so as soon as it was completed in the summer of 1939 Ingrid returned to Stockholm, to Petter and Pia, and to a film about a female chemist falling in love with a faithless sailor: *Juninatten*, released in 1940, was to be Ingrid's last film on home territory for more than a quarter of a century. By the time of its release, war had broken out and Lindstrom had decided that though it was his duty to remain in Sweden, Ingrid and Pia would be better off in California where the success of the American *Intermezzo* meant that Selznick was now desperate to take up his option on another film.

The only trouble was that he couldn't find one; the idea of a movie *Saint Joan*, which was to recur at almost all the crisis points of Ingrid's later life, had already come up for the first time but been rejected on the grounds that 1940 was perhaps not an ideal historical moment at which to show the French and the British locked in mortal combat. The Selznick office made sure, however, that Ingrid's return to New York in the January of 1940 did not go unnoticed: 'Picture' wrote Bosley Crowther in the New York Times, 'the sweetheart of a Viking, freshly scrubbed with Ivory soap, eating peaches and cream from a Dresden china bowl on the first warm day of Spring atop a sea-scarred cliff, and you have a fair impression of Ingrid Bergman.' I have always thought it infinitely to Ingrid's credit that, after reading a welcome like that, she didn't get straight back even onto a boat headed for wartime Europe.

In fact she stayed in New York because Selznick, having failed to find her a suitable Hollywood script to follow up the triumph of *Intermezzo*, agreed to let her play opposite Burgess Meredith on Broadway in *Liliom* (the script that later became the musical *Carousel*), a job Bergman only got because the producer Vinton Freedley thought she was Signe Hasso, another Swedish actress newly arrived in America but with vastly more stage experience than the three months Ingrid had enjoyed in Stockholm.

Nevertheless her reviews were good, and by the time she got back to Los Angeles in the autumn of 1940 Selznick had lined up a couple of tear-stained dramas for her: first *Adam Had Four Sons* with Warner Baxter, and then *Rage in Heaven* with Robert Montgomery saying 'if she had her way, she'd make the whole world happy'. In three initial Hollywood films Ingrid had thus far been cast as a nice pianist, a nice governess and a nice refugee: already there was a danger of a promising movie career being drowned at birth in treacle, thougggh as usual that was a danger which Bergman perceived well ahead of Selznick. He was about to loan her out again to MGM, this time to play the 'nice' Victorian fiancee to the *Dr Jekyll and Mr Hyde* of Spencer Tracy while Lana Turner played the 'not nice' barmaid of his alter ego romance. Bergman, circumventing the Selznick office, went straight to the film's director Victor Fleming with a more interesting propositon: why didn't she play the barmaid while Lana Turner, in a similar feat of counter-casting, played the fiancée? Fleming saw the intelligence of that, and her career was at last off the ground in America: within the next few months she played one of the great Garbo roles, *Anna Christie*, on stage in Santa Barbara and was then, she thought, set to return to cameras as the Spanish peasant Maria for whom the earth moves in *For Whom The Bell Tolls*. Hemingway had already given an interview to *Life* magazine stating that Ingrid was his ideal casting, but both had reckoned without the Paramount Studios contract-artist stable, in which there happened to be a Norwegian dancer called Vera Zorina who had to be found work.

It was therefore Zorina who started to shoot *For Whom The Bell Tolls*, and Bergman who went East with the stage version of *Anna Christie* and then settled in Rochester, New York, where Lindstrom was doing a two-year hospital training course in order to get his American medical qualifications. By now their differences intemperament, and Ingrid's new-found independence as a Hollywood movie star, was already causing cracks in the marriage, and Ingrid's temper was not greatly improved by the loss of the Hemingway, nor by the fact that in return for buying her the screen rights in *Gaslight* (which she had just seen on Broadway and badly wanted to film) Selznick was now insisting that she sign the dreaded seven-year contract.

The first picture under the new deal was however wonderfully fortunate: as soon as she had signed, Selznick flew her back to Hollywood from Rochester and lent her out to Warner Brothers, where they were desperate for a foreign star to take over a role that had already been turned down by Ann Sheridan and Hedy Lamarr – that of a European 'woman of mystery' who walks into a nightclub in wartime Casablanca.

As time went by, word quickly spread around the studio backlots that Warners had, more by luck than judgement, found themselves something special: a new and mysterious and romantic Bergman, quite different from the Viking lady of earlier and icier work. That word spread as far as Paramount, where they were by now in deep trouble with *For Whom The Bell Tolls*: Hemingway, they had reluctantly come to realise, had been right about his own book. It did need the Bergman they could now see in the early rushes of *Casablanca*. Selznick immediately put her price up to a hundred and fifty thousand dollars, and promptly lent her out again as the replacement for Zorina who had by now been ignominiously released from the film.

Within a few 1942 months, Ingrid was therefore to make two of the most commercially and critically triumphant movies of her entire career: 'Miss Bergman', wrote the great American movie critic James Agee at this time, 'not only bears a startling resemblance to an imaginable human being: she really knows how to act, in a blend of poetic grace with quiet realism which almost never appears in American pictures.'

But one of the problems with working in American pictures was of course that scripts like *Casablanca* and *For Whom The Bell Tolls* did not come along every day, and sometimes not even every decade. With both safely in the can she went on to *Saratoga Trunk*, yet another project for which she was about the third choice (this time after Bette Davis and Vivien Leigh had both turned it down) but one which would reunite her with Gary Cooper from the Hemingway and give her the refreshingly unusual role of a Creole adventuress. For contractual reasons Warner's then proceeded to keep this movie under wraps for fully two years before giving it a cautious release.

From there she went on to the *Gaslight* that Selznick had finally managed to get for her from the clutches of Irene Dunne and Hedy Lamarr, who were both after it; as the Victorian wife being driven slowly mad by Charles Boyer (as the husband after her fortune) Ingrid here got her first Oscar in 1944, even though it did look faintly like an apology for not giving her one in the previous year for either *Casablanca* or *For Whom The Bell Tolls*.

By now she was at the very height of her Hollywood career: from *Gaslight* she turned into a nun for the hugely successful *Bells of St Mary's*, Bing Crosby's follow-up to *Going My Way* in which he was yet again cast as a twinkling Irish priest, and for that she (or rather Selznick under the terms of her exclusive contract) earned a quarter of a million dollars. By now there was a joke around New York which ran 'Guess what I saw today? A picture not starring Ingrid Bergman', but the lady herself was getting more than a little irritated with the way that Selznick would simply farm her out to the highest studio bidder and keep a sizeable chunk of the resulting profit without seriously planning or apparently taking much personal interest in the shape of Bergman's postwar career, while she herself was still on the flat-rate two thousand dollars a week.

Under pressure from both the Lindstroms, he therefore now brought her together with his other great contract artist of the period, Alfred Hitchcock, for the first and most successful of the three films they were to make together over the next three years: *Spellbound* cast her opposite Gregory Peck, she as the psychiatrist and he as the suspiciously amnesiac director of the clinic where she works. At once it was clear that Hitchcock had found another of the fire-beneath-ice blondes that were to characterise his Hollywood work from Joan Fontaine through thirty years to Grace Kelly, and *Spellbound* was such a success that Selznick immediately moved Bergman and Hitchcock on towards *Notorious*. In the interval between the two films she went to Paris as part of a war's-end army concert troupe, and there fell passionately in love with the photographer Robert Capa.

She would, she said later, have asked Lindstrom for a divorce and married Capa had the latter shown any desire to marry her, but like all great war photographers he was a quintessential loner, and Bergman therefore returned somewhat unhappily to Hollywood and Hitchcock. *Notorious* was to be made by much the same production team as *Spellbound*, though with Cary Grant in place of Gregory Peck and a vastly more complex counter-espionage plot which required her to play a hard-drinking spy feigning interest in a leading South American Nazi (Claude Rains) but eventually of course falling for Cary. The film was ecstatically received around the world, and Ingrid was not to know that it was to be her last success for a decade.

Her contract with Selznick was now drawing to a close, and both she and Lindstrom (who still looked after her business affairs even though their private ones were clearly also nearing an end) decided that this was the moment to capitalise on her immense box-office success and go independent. 'Ah Ingrid,' said Hitchcock ruefully when he heard of this plan, 'so beautiful, so stupid'. The idea was that, as the top box-office female star of the late 1940s, she would now do better choosing her own scripts and co-stars, an idea that was rapidly disproved by the first one she chose: *Arch of Triumph*, though it co-starred Charles Boyer from *Gaslight* and boasted 'additional dialogue by Bertolt Brecht', was a curious disaster which managed to lose two million dollars at the box office.(some of that Ingrid's) but retains a sharp historical interest in that the story by Erich Maria Remarque of a doctor falling in love with a cabaret star just as the Nazis were entering Paris was in fact loosely based on his own prewar affair there with Marlene Dietrich. American cinema audiences of 1948 were not however much interested in that kind of history, and the collapse of *Arch of Triumph* served almost immediately to destroy Ingrid's box-office magic.

She then went back to Broadway to play the *Saint Joan* she had always promised herself, not in the Shaw script which she thought 'too clever' but in a lacklustre version by Maxwell Anderson called *Joan of Lorraine* which did all right on stage but proved another loser when she filmed it in Hollywood a few months later. What she badly needed then, after *Joan* and *Arch of Triumph*, was a big commercial success and the man to give it to her was surely the Hitchcock with whom she had recently worked so

7

well on *Notorious* and *Spellbound*. Sadly however her run of ill-luck seemed to be catching, and *Under Capricorn* turned out to be a desperately overlong and static saga of 1830s Australian outback life: the same Bosley Crowther who had welcomed her to New York in such ecstatically over-the-top terms eight years earlier now noted in the *New York Times* 'Miss Bergman is called upon for soggy displays of sozzled and sentimental maundering or wide-eyed and dry-throated dread'.

But there was worse to come; much worse. At about this time, Ingrid had wandered into a Los Angeles cinema one night (possibly the same one she had visited in search of 'the real Bogart' during their filming of *Casablanca*) and seen a film that was to change her life. Rossellini's *Rome Open City* had been made on location in the last days of the war: no studios, no actors, just the beginning of a whole new world of realist cinema. A few weeks later Ingrid saw another of his films, *Paisan* and on the strength of that wrote him her famous request for work: 'if you need a Swedish actress who speaks English very well, has not forgotten her German, who is not very understandable in French and who in Italian knows only 'Ti amo', I am ready to come and make a film with you.'

In the light of the furore which ensued, it needs to be remembered that she had at this time never met Rossellini and therefore her 'ti amo' was merely a phrase from a foreign-language manual, not a declaration of any personal love. Though it might as well have been: by March 1949, less than two years after posting that letter, she was in Rome filming and living with the Italian director. To understand how all this could possibly have happened so fast, you have to understand what Rossellini represented to Bergman: not just a director she admired, but an escape from a dead marriage, a studio system she was finding increasingly unreal, and a country where she had gone from five initial years of consistent success to two of total disaster. Ingrid was now thirty-three, in need of a new life and a new career and maybe a new country. Rossellini offered all of that, and Ingrid took the offer without, I suspect, the faintest idea of what her acceptance would mean in America.

Ingrid was not, after all, American: she had merely lived there for rather less than a decade and made a dozen movies of which half had been major hits. It was, in her view, a business arrangement that she had made with the United States: her roots were still in Sweden. That was not quite how Hollywood saw it. In their most isolationist time, at the start of the McCarthy years, here was the girl they had made into a world star running off with some Italian. Abandoning her husband and daughter was maybe bad enough; but Bergman was also abandoning the studios, the American film industry and all that was held most sacred in Los Angeles to work with some guy who didn't even build sets or speak English or use actors. What kind of betrayal was this?

Even so, she might just have managed to get away with it (others including Katharine Hepburn had from time to time turned their backs on Hollywood only to be welcomed home when the studios really needed them) had it not been made abundantly clear by the Italian press in August 1949 that Bergman was not merely living and filming with Rossellini in Italy but also now pregnant by him. This somehow seemed to confirm all Hollywood's worst fears about foreign film directors who worked away from their studios in strange languages, and Ingrid was now pilloried and destroyed by the American press as only Chaplin and Fatty Arbuckle had been in the past.

Matters were not much helped by the fact that her film of *St Joan* was by now on release, nor by the fact that Lindstrom, who might in happier circumstances have given her a quick and quiet divorce, was understandably enraged at having just been denied a good hospital job because of his albeit innocent 'involvement' in what was now called 'the Bergman affair'. He therefore took the view that in running off to Rossellini Ingrid had ruined more lives than her own, not least his and possibly Pia's: the access fight was long and nasty, as was the divorce, and by the end of it Ingrid's American career was deep in the ashes that were all too symbolically strewn around *Stromboli*, her first Rossellini film and one set on a volcanic island.

By 14 March 1950, soon after the birth out of wedlock of Ingrid's only Rossellini son, a Senator Johnson was having read into the formal historical record of the US Senate a speech which concluded 'if, out of the degradation associated with *Stromboli*, decency and common sense can be established in Hollywood then Ingrid Bergman will not have destroyed her career for naught. Out of her ashes may come a better Hollywood.' It was considerably to the credit of another senator, Charles Percy, that in April 1972 he managed to get the record of that shameful speech adjusted, and entered instead a tribute to Ingrid's integrity at a time of persecution. 'My war with America', Ingrid noted, 'was over long ago, but the wounds remained; now, because of that gallant gesture, they are healed forever.'

But that healing took another twenty years: in the meantime, cut off from her daughter and her career in America, Bergman eventually married Rossellini and gave birth to two more of his children, twin girls. It was soon all too clear, however, that as a professional partnership theirs was less than wonderful: Ingrid's strong studio training in both Stockholm and Hollywood was of no use at all in coping with Rossellini's free-fall documentary style of streetcorner shooting, and even if she herself had been any longer acceptable at American box-offices it is extremely doubtful whether any of her Rossellini films would have been. Even now, when Rossellini is being taught in American university film schools, it would be a brave cinema manager who tried to open *Stromboli* at a cinema in the Mid-West or indeed the middle of England.

It would be quite wrong, though, to assume that Ingrid was therefore desperately unhappy at the loss of her old American audience or her failure to find a new Italian one. In the Spring of 1953, my father was working on the film of *Beat the Devil* in Italy: its other stars were Jennifer Jones (who had followed Bergman as Selznick's principal contract star and was now also his wife) and Humphrey Bogart, with whom a decade earlier Ingrid had made *Casablanca*: not surprisingly therefore she drove the few miles from her Rossellini home to the location to meet up with her old friends from California. That was the first time I ever met her, and home movies of the period show a remarkably cheerful lady. Bogart, she told me years later, had enquired at that reunion how she could possibly have given everything up for Rossellini: 'I told him well, I am now a very happy woman, and maybe that is just as important as being a box-office success in America.' I doubt that Bogart believed her about the success, but about the happiness there could not have been much doubt.

It didn't last, though; a succession of increasingly unloved and unsuccessful Rossellini movies and a catastrophic stage tour of Honegger's *Joan of Arc* oratorio, which ended with Ingrid being booed in her native Stockholm, took their toll of a marriage which had been under near-intolerable strain since the very beginning, and by 1955 it was clear that the Italian adventure was over both professionally and romantically.

It was then that Jean Renoir came up with what looked like the ideal escape for Ingrid: still appalled by the way Hollywood had treated a star he considered of bright and particular radiance, he built her a lyrical romantic screen comedy called *Elena et les Hommes* and invited her to make it in Paris. Though it was never a commercial success, the sight of Bergman in Paris working with the great Renoir somehow brought her back into the viewfinders of directors who had thought her lost to Rossellini forever. One of those was Anatole Litvak, then about to make *Anastasia* in England but for an American company. He had, he told them, now found the ideal star in Ingrid, and would not indeed even consider making the picture without her. Twentieth Century Fox were appalled: true, the Hollywood climate had loosened up considerably in the five years that she had spent with Rossellini, and divorces and even children born out of wedlock were now not exactly unknown amid the Hollywood hills. But Bergman was still high on the hit-list of the gossip columnists (most of whom mainly resented the fact that she had allowed her 'scandalous' pregnancy to hit the Italian papers before their own) and some way would now have to be found to get her back into favour if *Anastasia* was not to be a total disaster.

A suitable compromise was soon reached: Litvak would be allowed to cast her as the mysterious claimant to the Russian throne provided the Grand Duchess was played by the actress then and now billed as 'first lady of the American stage', Helen Hayes. By being seen side by side on screen, it was thought that something of Miss Hayes' legendary probity and dignity would then rub off on Ingrid: in an almost royal way, audiences could then be persuaded that if Miss Hayes had deigned to be seen in public with her, perhaps she might be all right again.

And so it proved: *Anastasia* was a huge success, and Ingrid immediately followed it with an equally triumphant Parisian stage debut in *Tea and Sympathy*. She got a divorce from Rossellini that, given his histrionic temperament, was very nearly as stormy as their elopement and then married (for the third and last time) her producer on *Tea and Sympathy*, the Swedish theatrical impresario Lars Schmidt.

Anastasia brought her a second Oscar in 1957, and when she went to claim it she found (like Chaplin twenty years later) that Hollywood seemed to have forgotten all its old hostility even if she couldn't. They still weren't about to let her film that close to her old home, however: her next assignment (a leaden light comedy called *Indiscreet* which did at least manage to reunite her with Cary Grant) was carefully shot in London, which had now become her second home while she and Schmidt set up a residence in France.

Under Schmidt's intelligent management, she also began to realise that films weren't the only way for an actress to make a living: more and more now she began turning towards the stage and television for classical work ranging from *Hedda Gabler* to O'Neill's *More Stately Mansions* and Shaw's *Captain Brassbound's Conversion*, finding often in the West End the critical acceptance as a distinguished actress that had always been denied her in the cinema.

Her films were still rather more hit-or-miss however: after *Anastasia* she had her last really big success in the 1958 *Inn of the Sixth Happiness* but then did a disappointing screen version of Sagan's *Aimez-Vous Brahms*? ('Brahms, oui' wrote one waspish Parisian reviewer) and a segment of a Swedish mistake called *Stimulantia* which was only justified by the chance it gave her to work one last time with her first great mentor Molander. Also in the sixties she did a disappointing screen version of *The Visit* and a bit which looked as though it had been written for Katharine Hepburn in an all-star compilation job called *The Yellow Rolls-Royce*.

8

It was clear by now that her interests were really focussed on the stage, and even when (on the strength of her Broadway success in *More Stately Mansions*) Columbia signed her to the first American contract she had had since Selznick, the films they provided her with (*Cactus Flower* and *A Walk in the Spring Rain*) were so feeble and unsuccessful that they might as well have not bothered.

In the 1970s she did more stage work in Chichester and London (Maugham's *The Constant Wife*, Hunter's *Waters of the Moon*) as well as a couple more undistinguished American films (*From The Mixed-Up Files of Mrs Basil Frankweiler* and *A Matter of Time*) as well as making her third Oscar-winning appearance, this one in the admittedly small role of the mad Swedish missionary on board the *Orient Express*. Her final assignments were happily rather more distinguished.

In 1978, divorced from Schmidt who was nonetheless to remain a loving friend, and already well aware that she was dying of cancer, she went to work for the first time with her Swedish namesake Ingmar Bergman: the film was *Autumn Sonata*, and in it Ingrid played a world-famous concert pianist who has neglected her family and specifically her daughter (Liv Ullmann) for the sake of a career that was vastly more important to her than family ties. If there were Rossellini overtones here, nobody on the film was tactless enough to mention them and Bergman gave in her last feature film one of her most haunting characterisations.

It was not however her last screen appearance: that was as Golda Meir in a two-part television film shot only months before her death in 1982. Working now in considerable pain and intense Israeli heat, with a script that was at best a conventional tele-biopic of the 'Famous Lives' variety, she yet managed to turn in a performance of considerable power and intelligence. She had become, just too late, a really good actress if not perhaps a great one: here's looking at you, kid.

SHERIDAN MORLEY

"The minute I looked at her, I knew I had something.
She had an extraordinary quality of purity and nobility
and a definite star personality that is very rare.
But she acted like a movie-struck teenager.
I remember having a party for her at my home.
Spencer Tracy, Charles Boyer, and a dozen other movie stars
were there. She just sat in a corner staring at them
in awe. She was so shy she couldn't stop blushing."

David O. Selznick

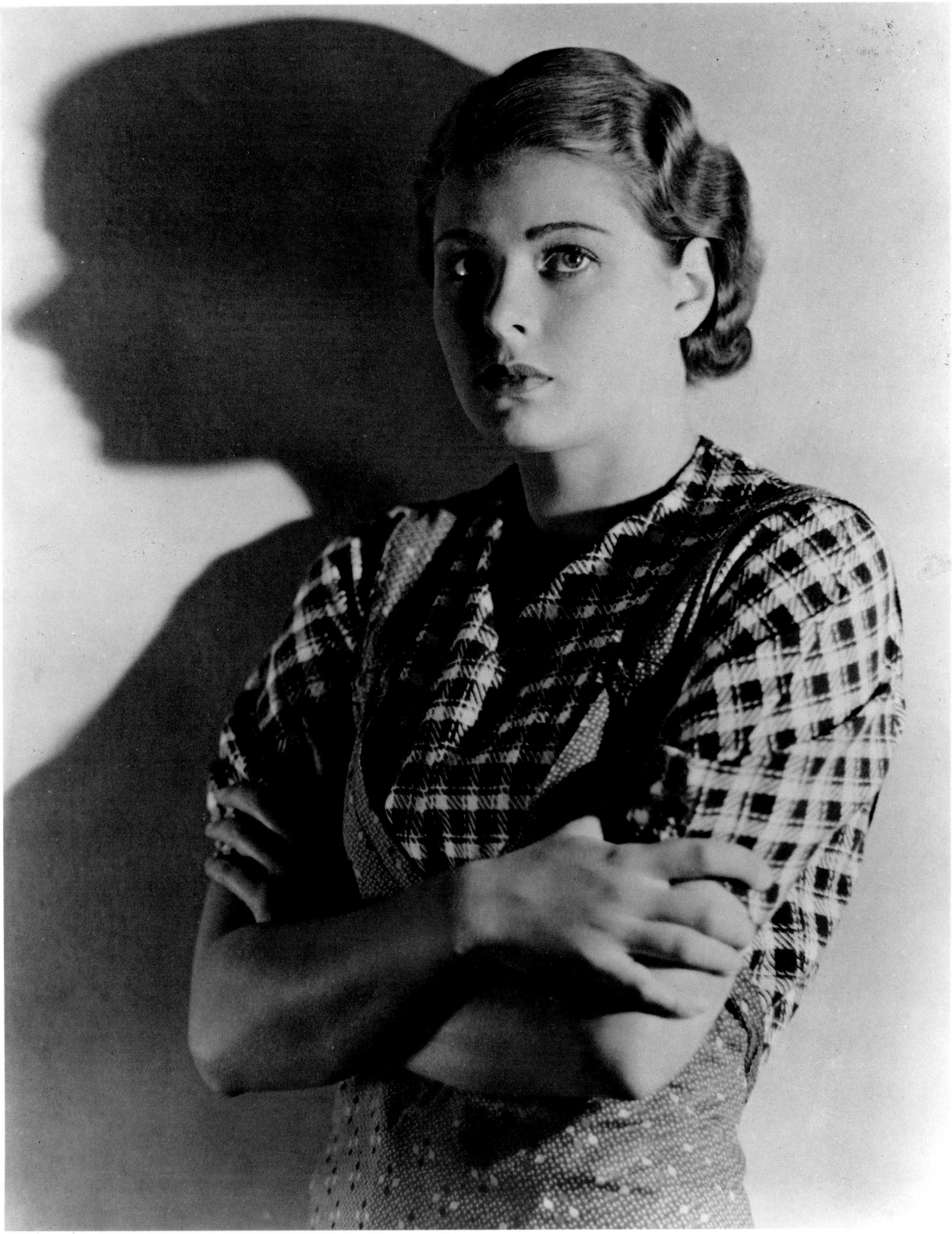

9

10

11

12

13

14

"It is unfair to call her a second Garbo,
just because she hails from Sweden.
She has a combination of rare beauty, freshness,
vitality and ability that is as uncommon
as a century plant in bloom."

Wanda Hale, reviewing *Intermezzo*

15

16

17

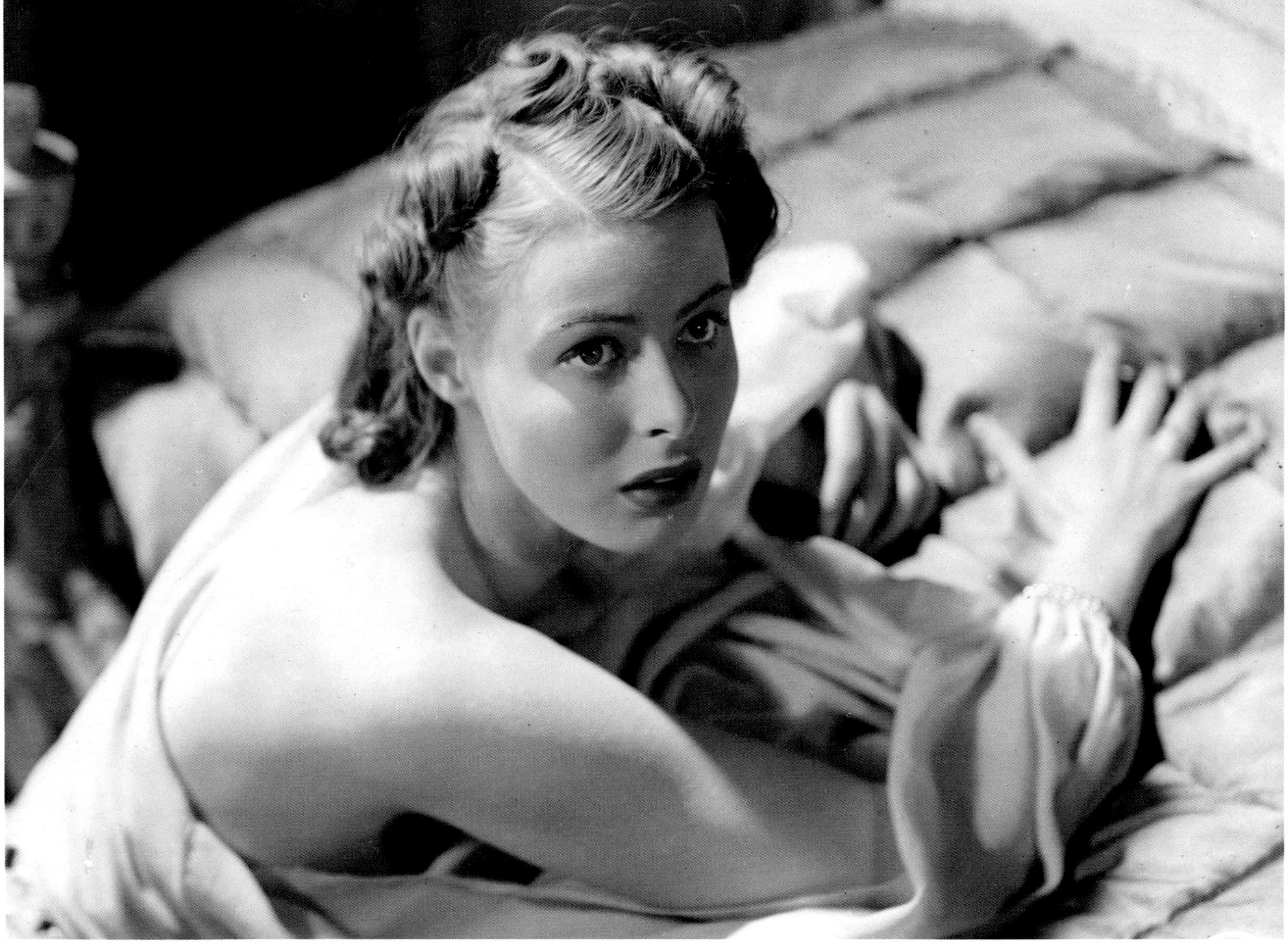

19

"What star before has made her first appearance
on the international screen with a highlight gleaming
on her nose tip? That gleam is typical of a performance
that doesn't give the effect of acting at all
but of living – without make-up."

Graham Greene reviewing *Intermezzo*

20

21

22

23

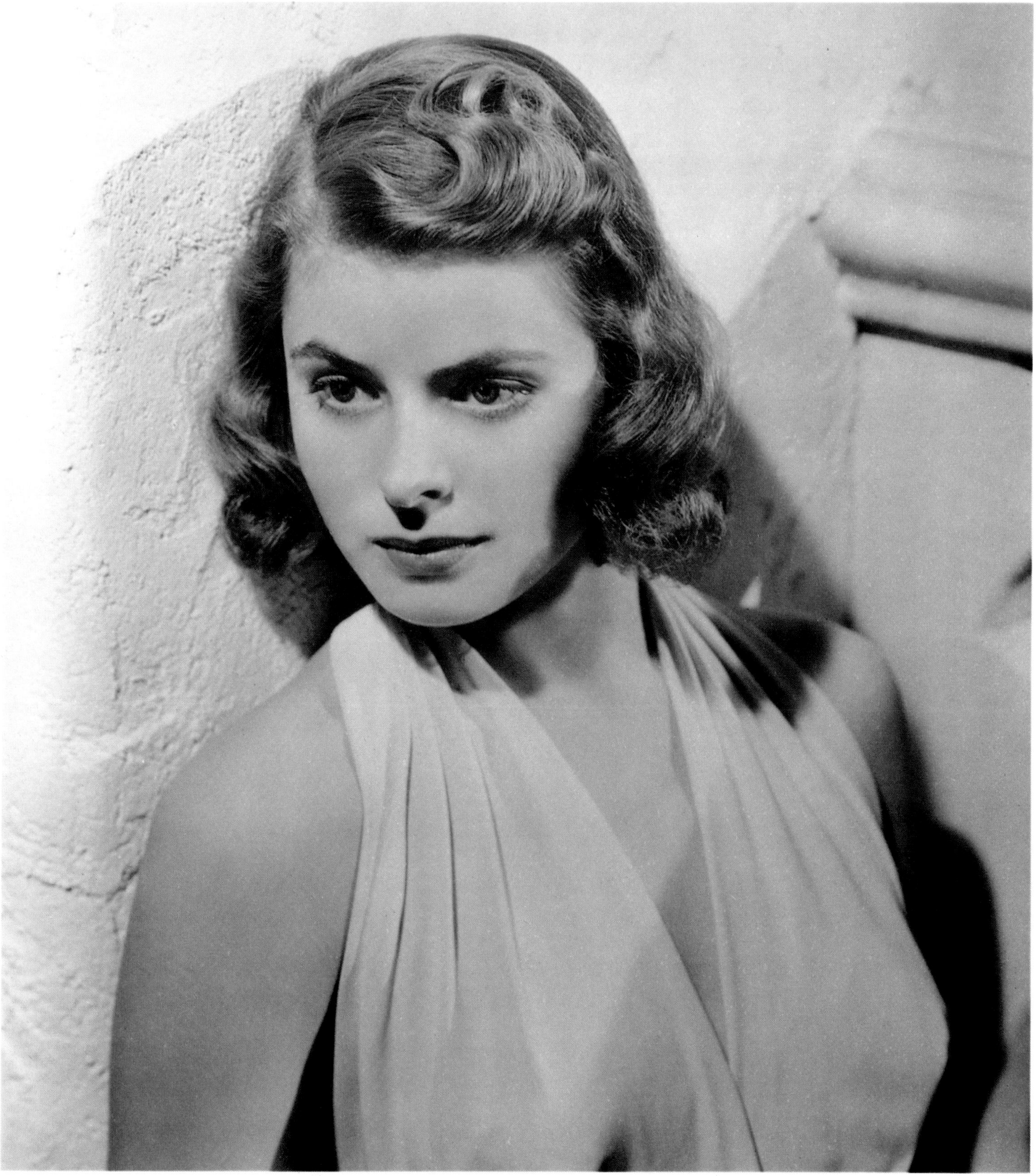

25

26

27

28

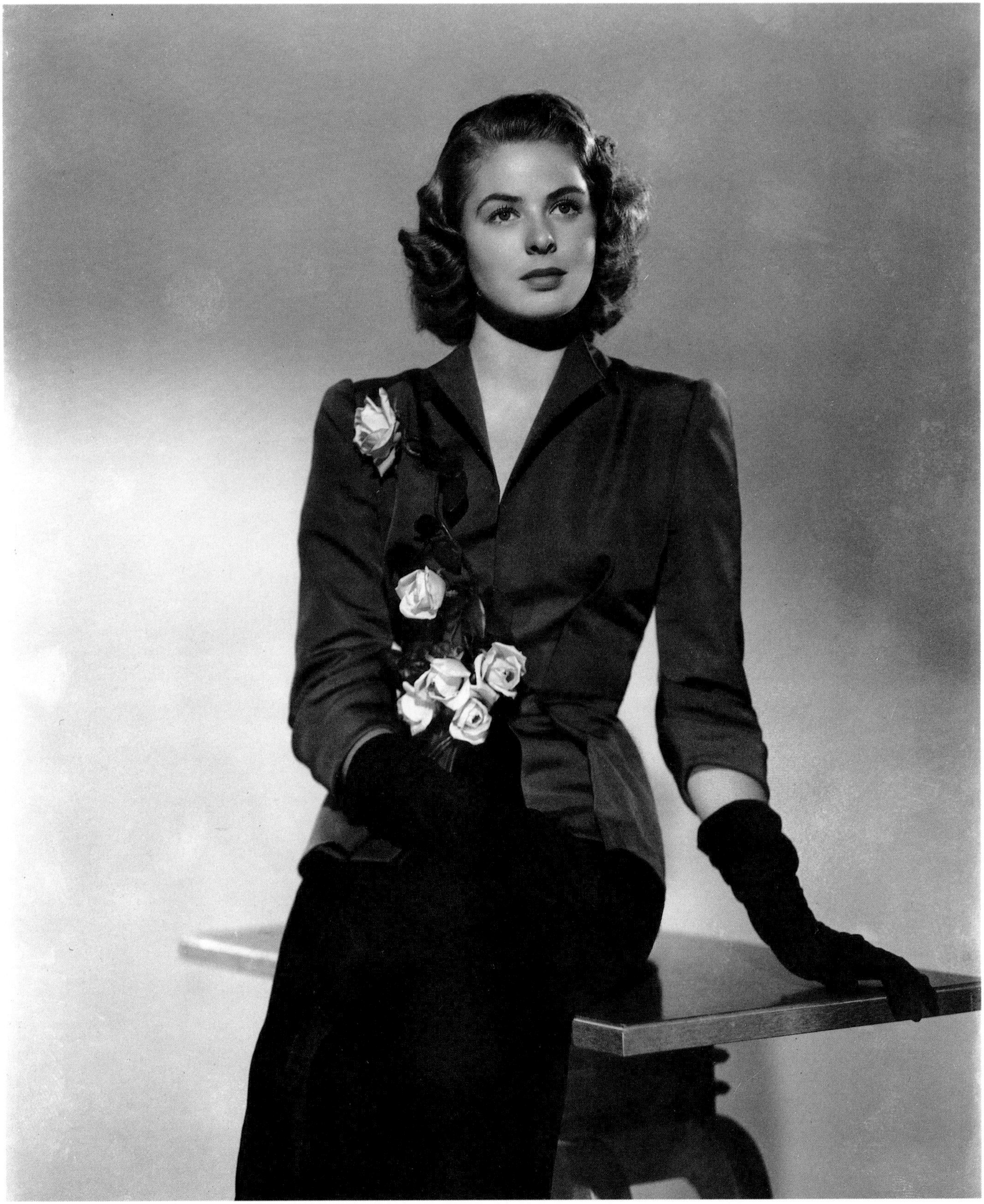

30

31

32

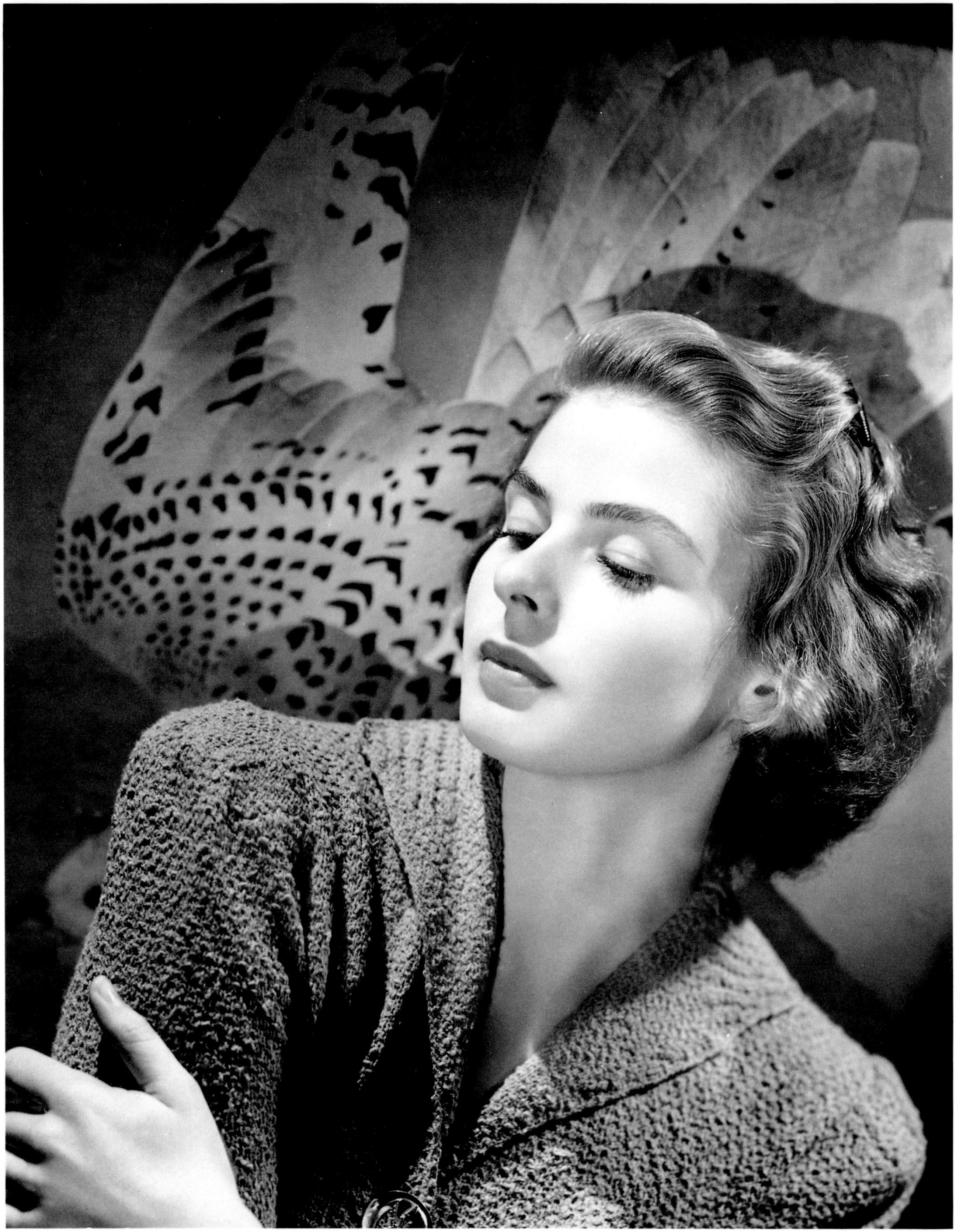

33

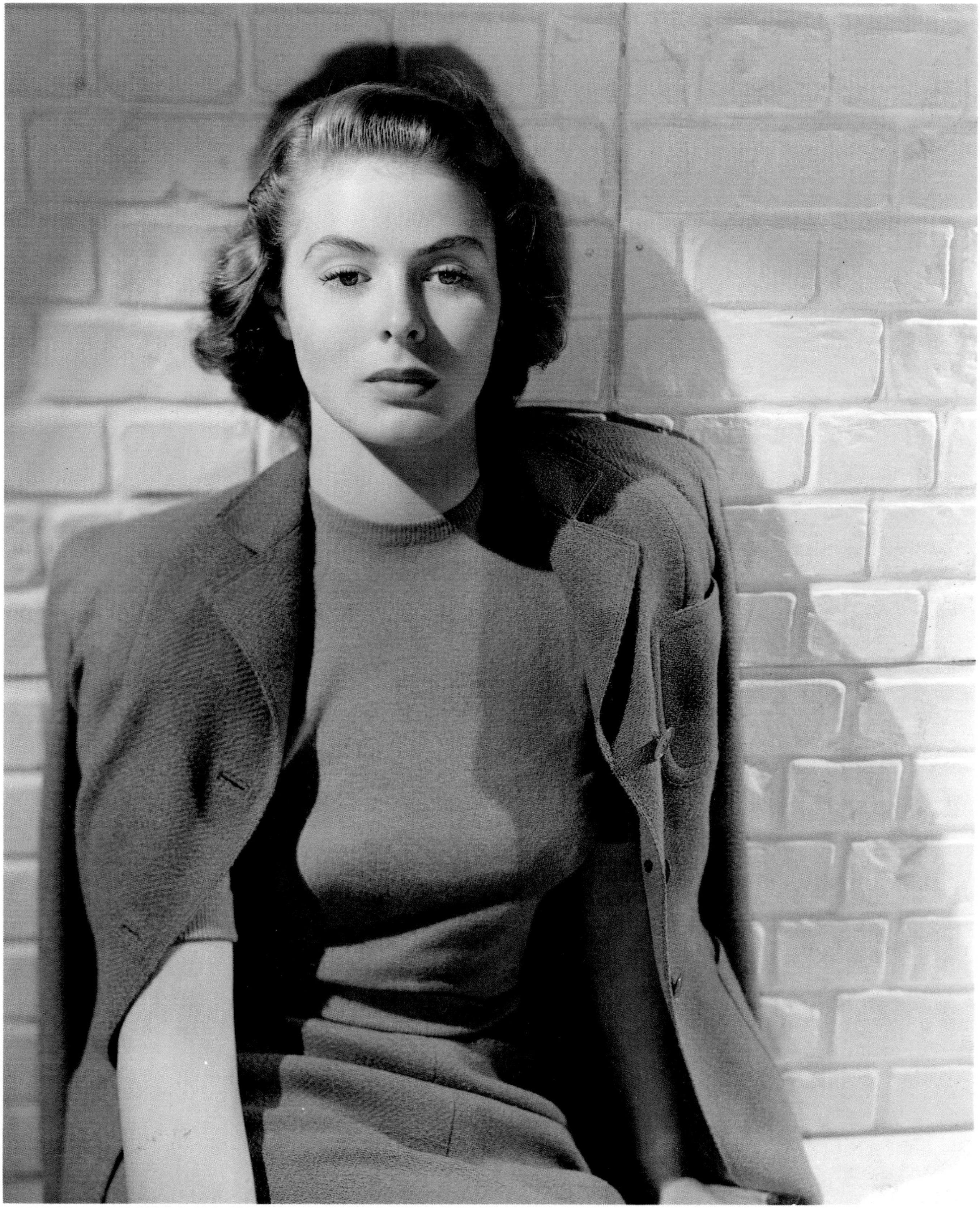

34

"Ah, Ingrid. So beautiful, so stupid . . ."
Alfred Hitchcock

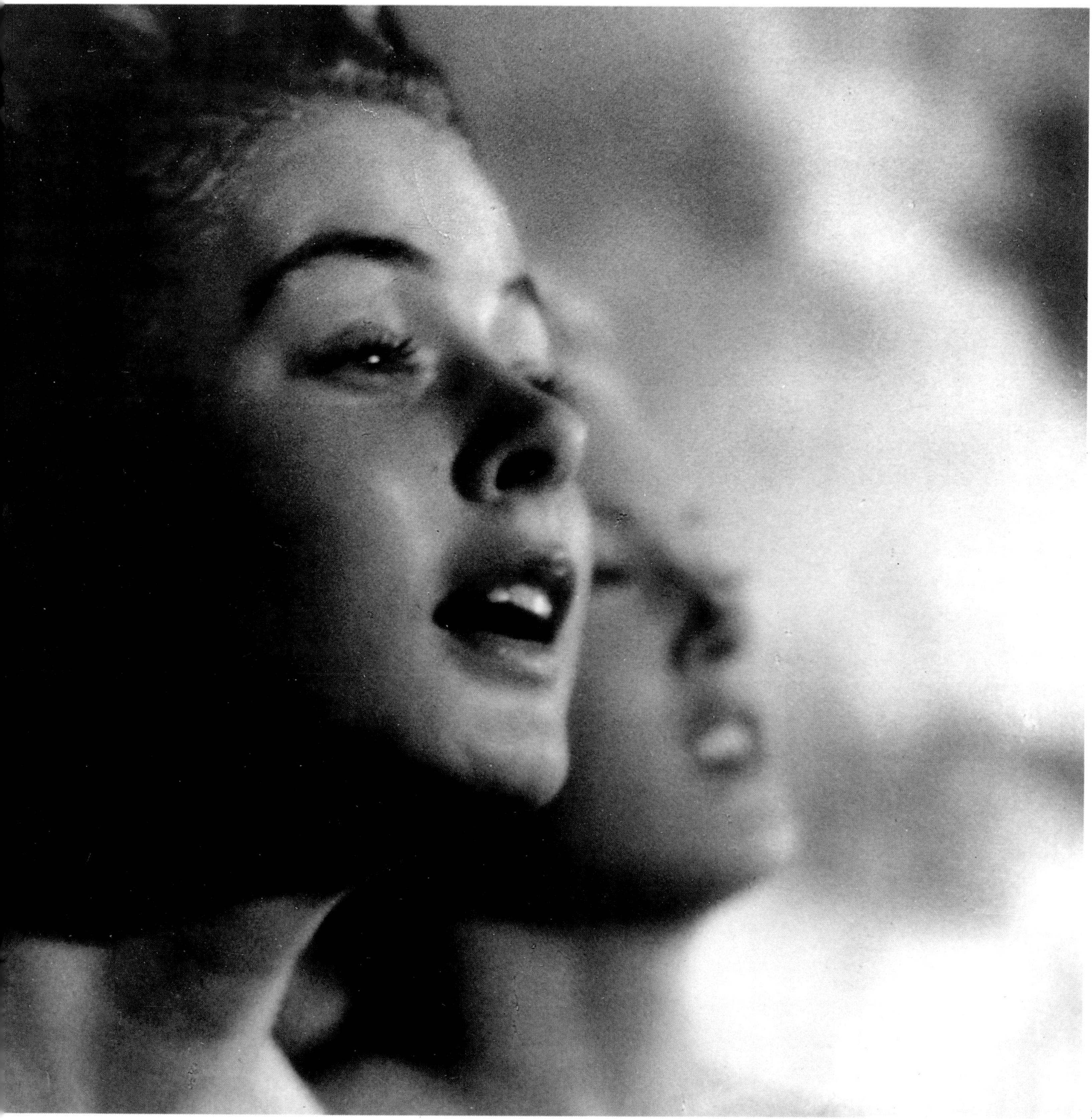

"Glamour. That's what (Casablanca's) lovely star had,
something out of this world,
far away; high up in the cinema's darkness.
Here's looking at you, kid."

Stanley Eveleny, The Scotsman

36

37

38

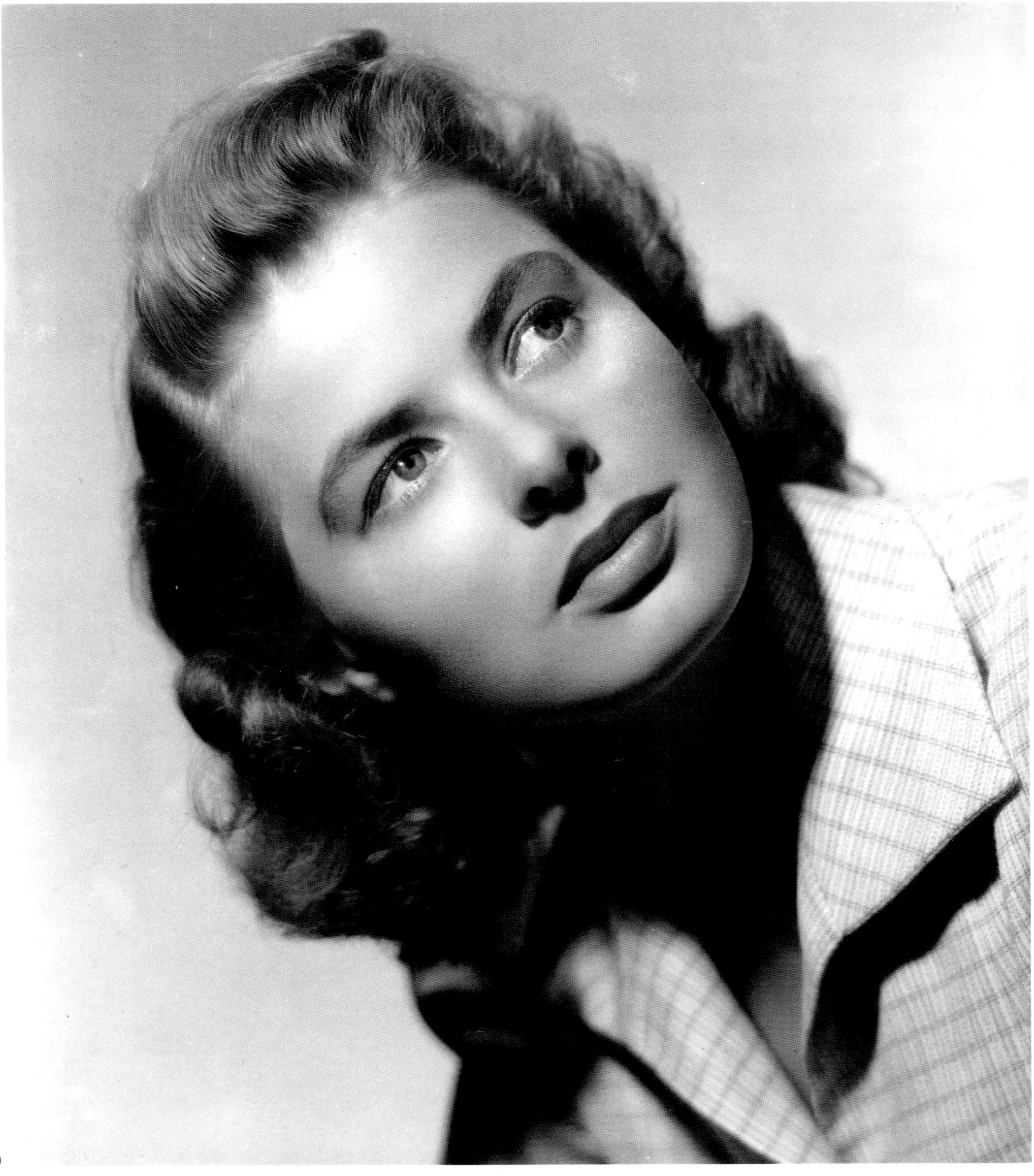

"Picture the sweetheart of a Viking,
freshly scrubbed with ivory soap,
eating peaches and cream from a Dresden china bowl
on the first warm day of spring atop a sea-scarred cliff,
and you have a fair impression of Ingrid Bergman."

Bosley Crowther, New York Times

40

41

42

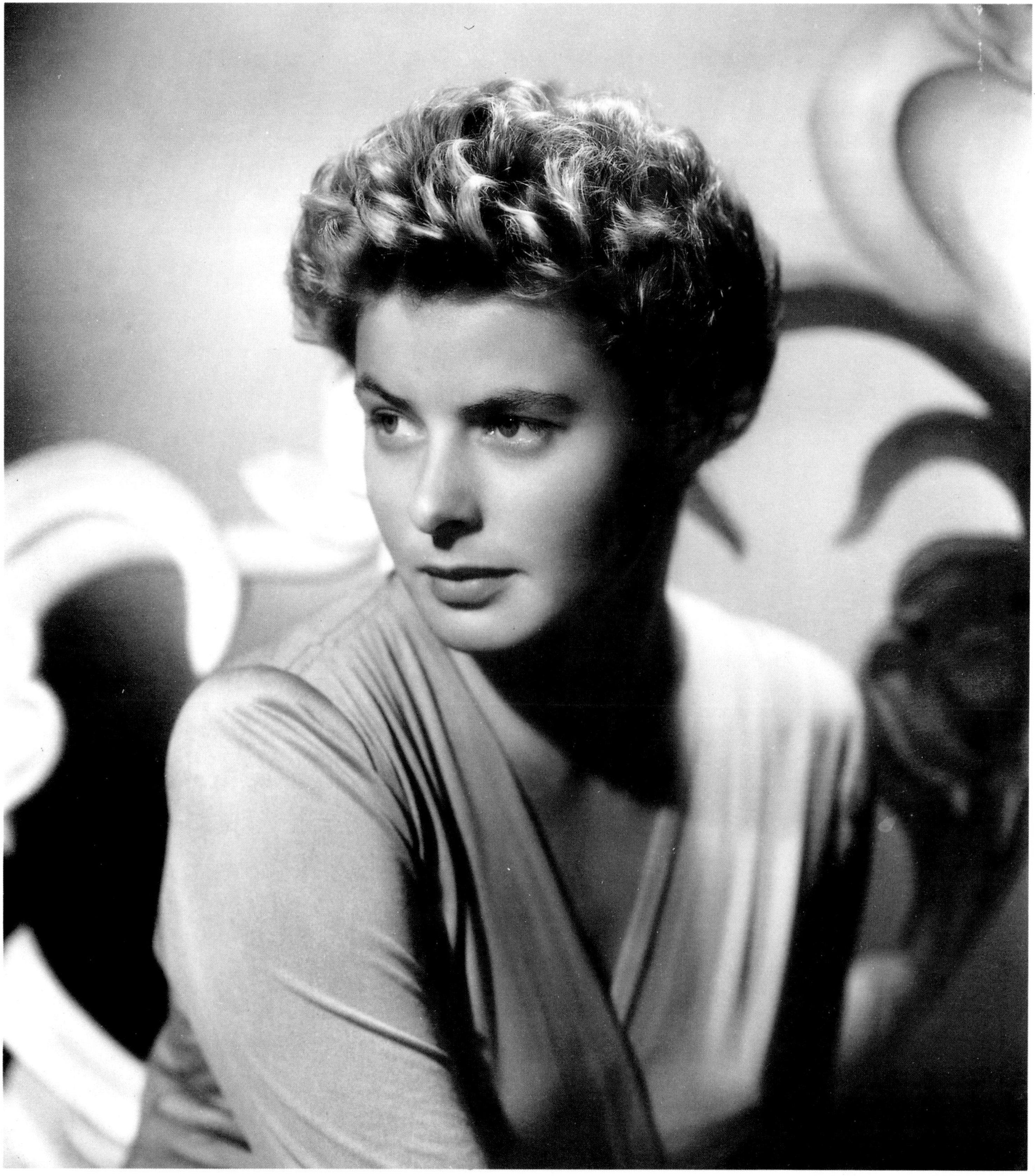

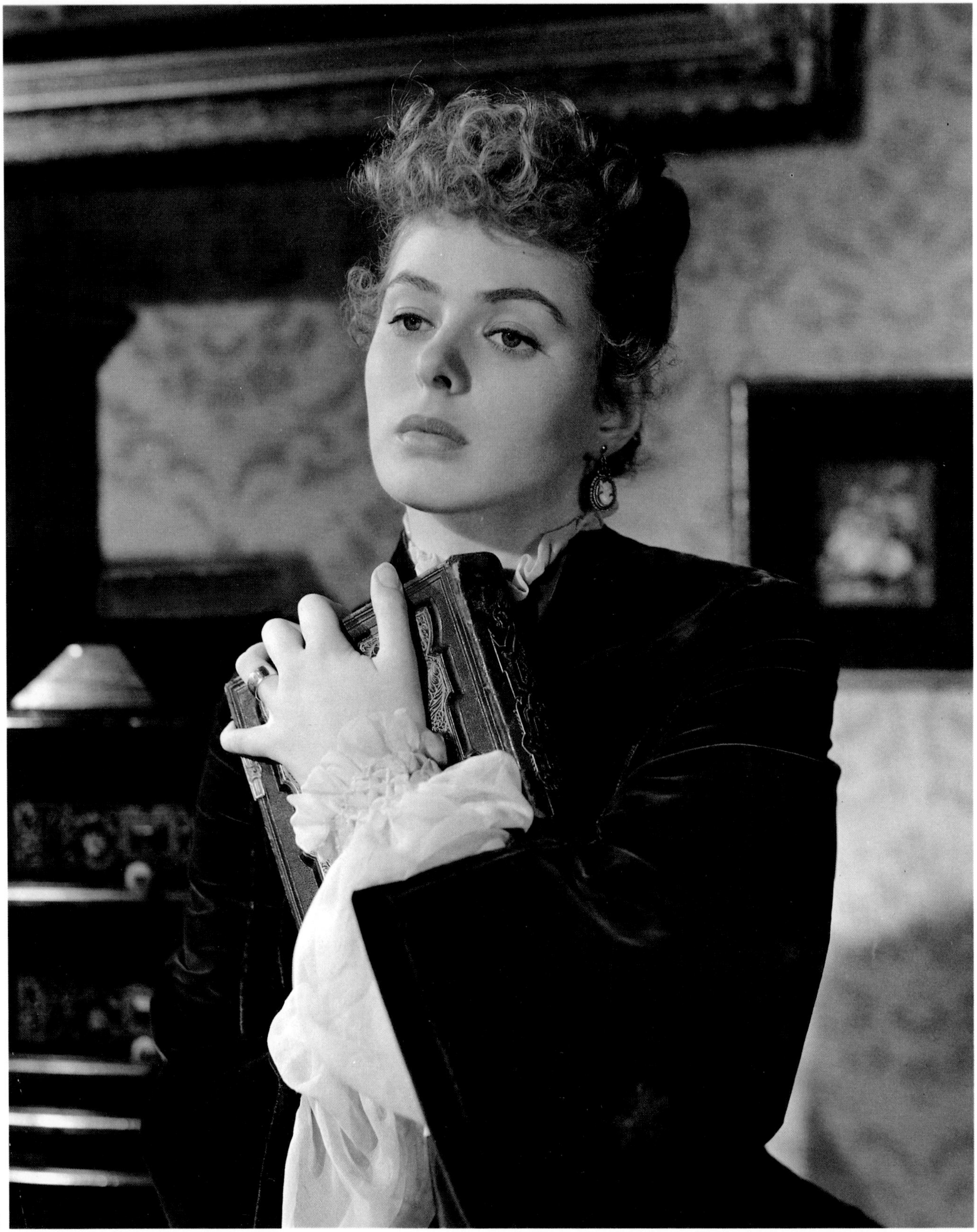

45

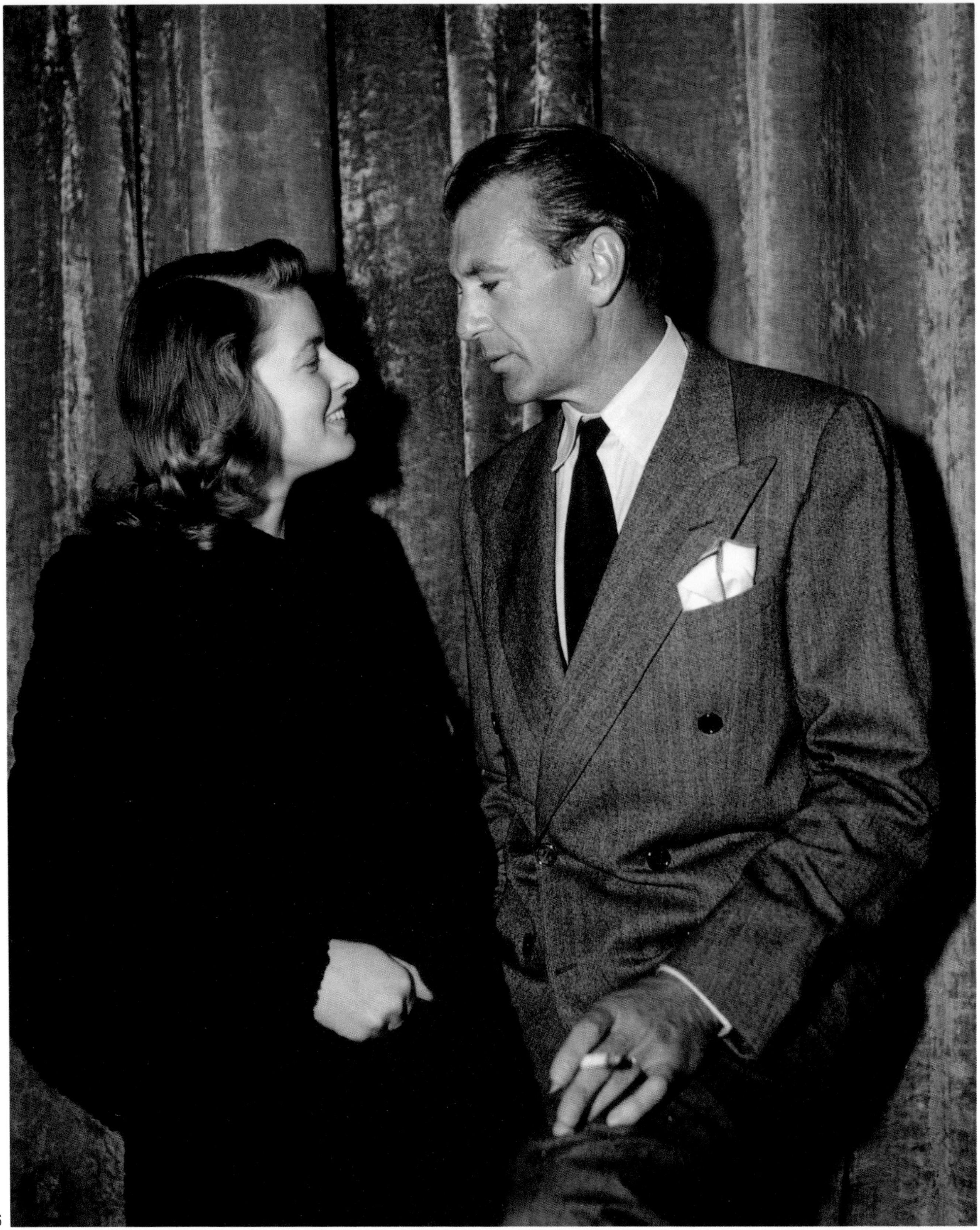

"We deliberately built her up
as the normal, healthy, non-neurotic career woman
devoid of scandal and with an idyllic home life.
I guess that backfired later."

David O. Selznick

47

48

49

50

Ingrid Bergman

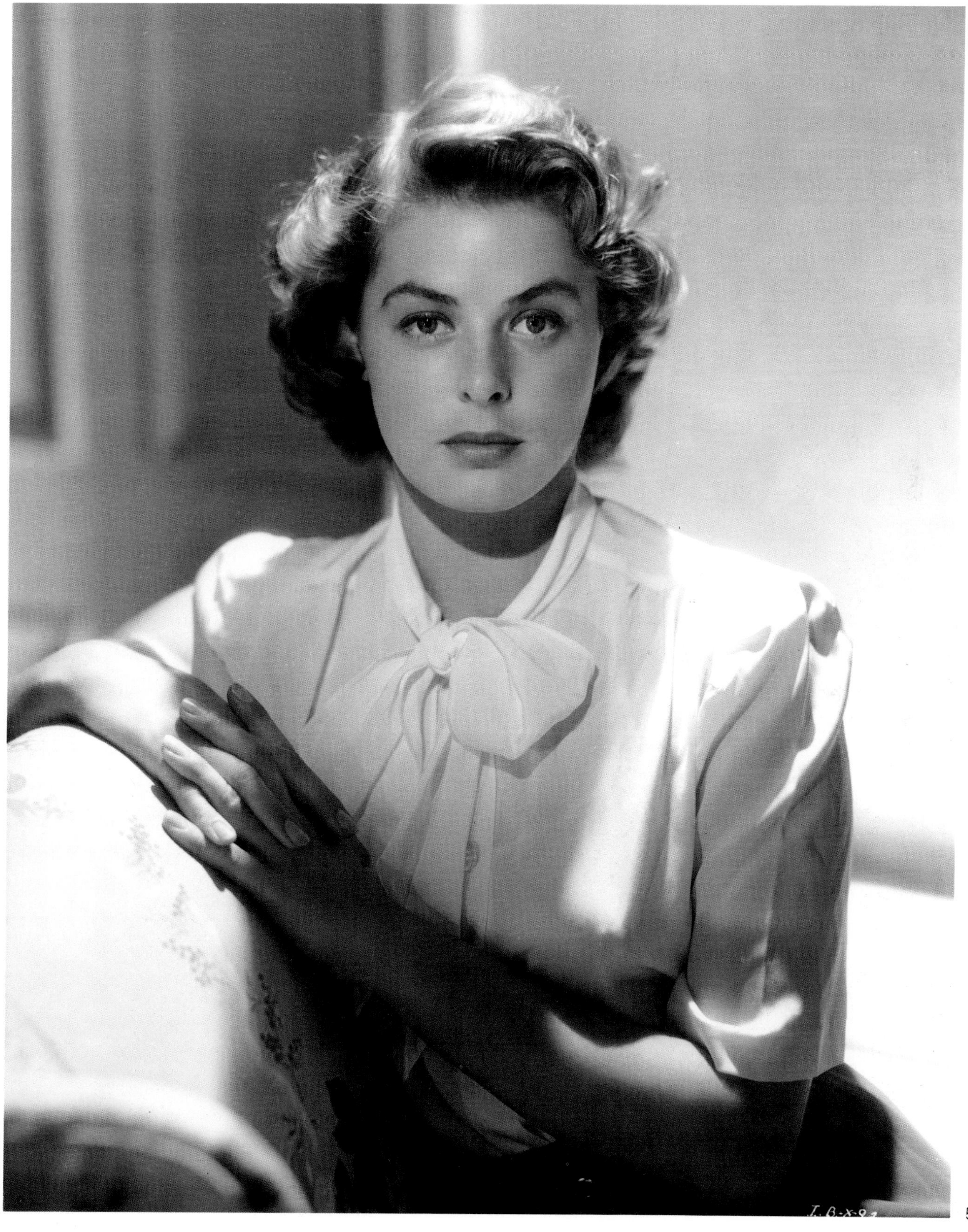

"Oh, but she's a woman's woman.
I mean, she is everything a woman should be.
She's the kind of woman men aren't afraid of because she's so warm.
She has a regal quality.
It's too bad she isn't a queen of some country."

Goldie Hawn

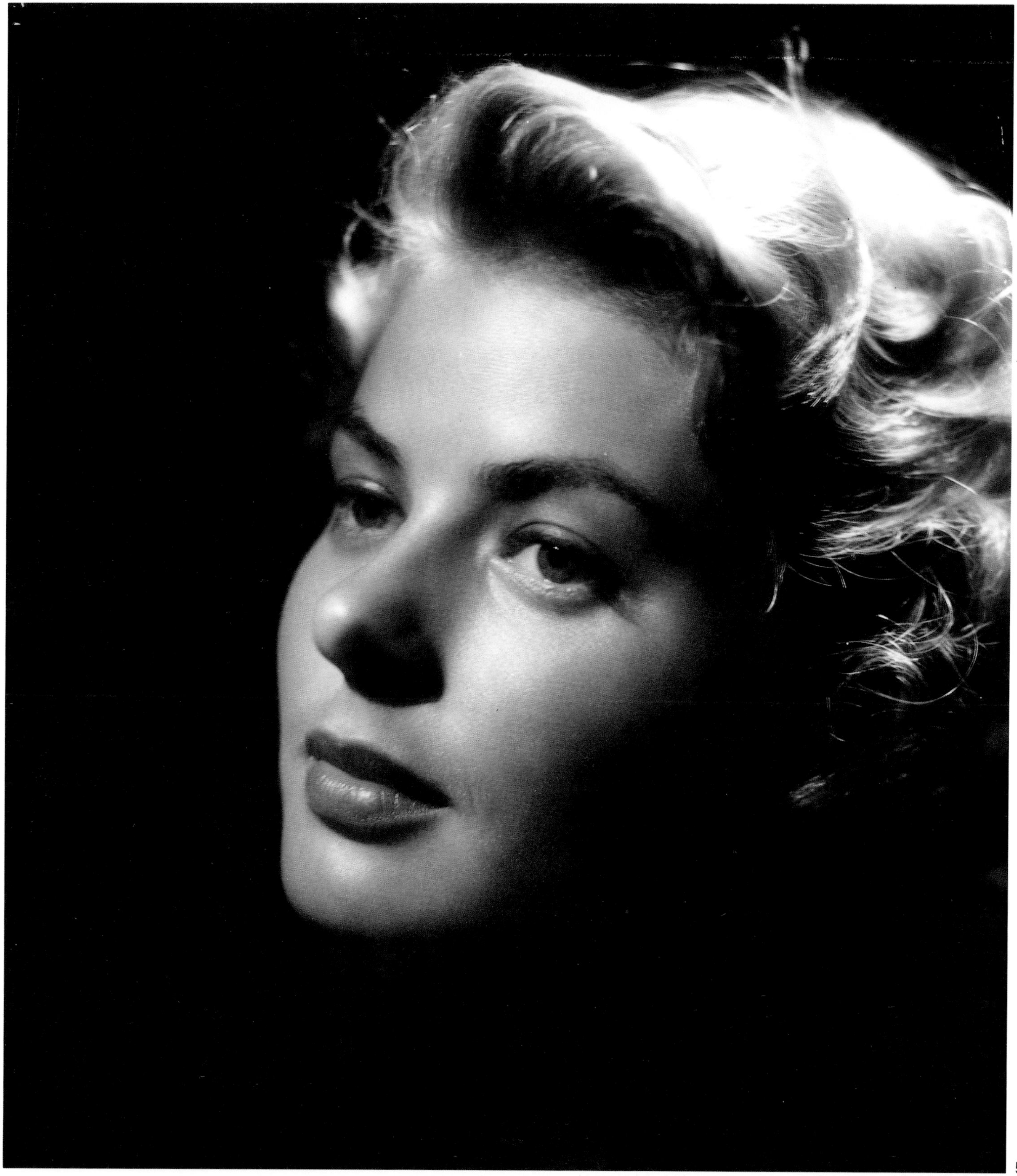

54

55

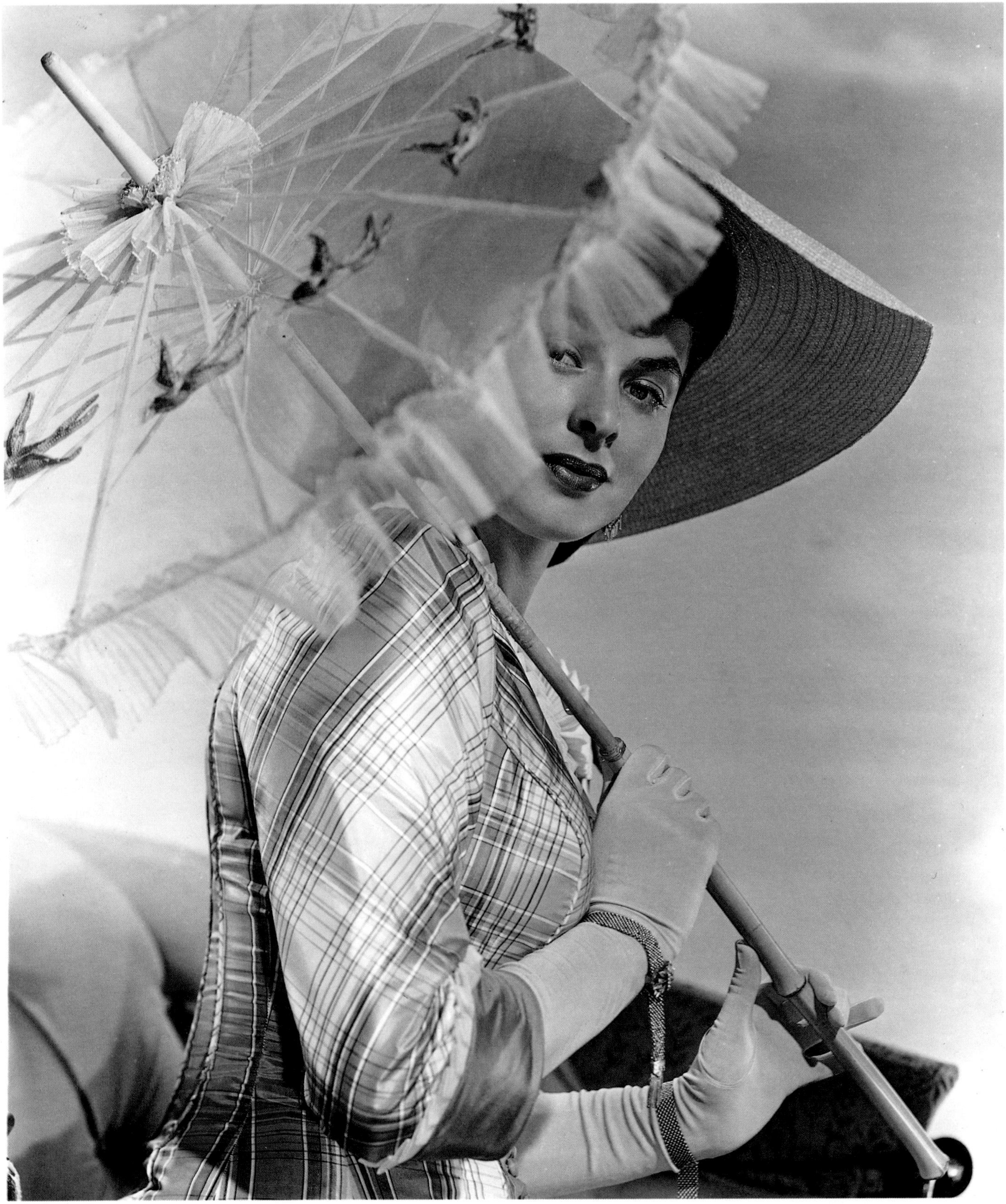

"Miss Bergman not only bears a startling resemblance
to an imaginable human being;
she really knows how to act, in a blend of poetic grace
with quiet realism which almost never appears in American pictures"

James Agee

57

58

59

"There are only seven movie stars in the world whose name alone will induce American bankers to lend money for movie productions, and the only woman on the list is Ingrid Bergman."

Cary Grant

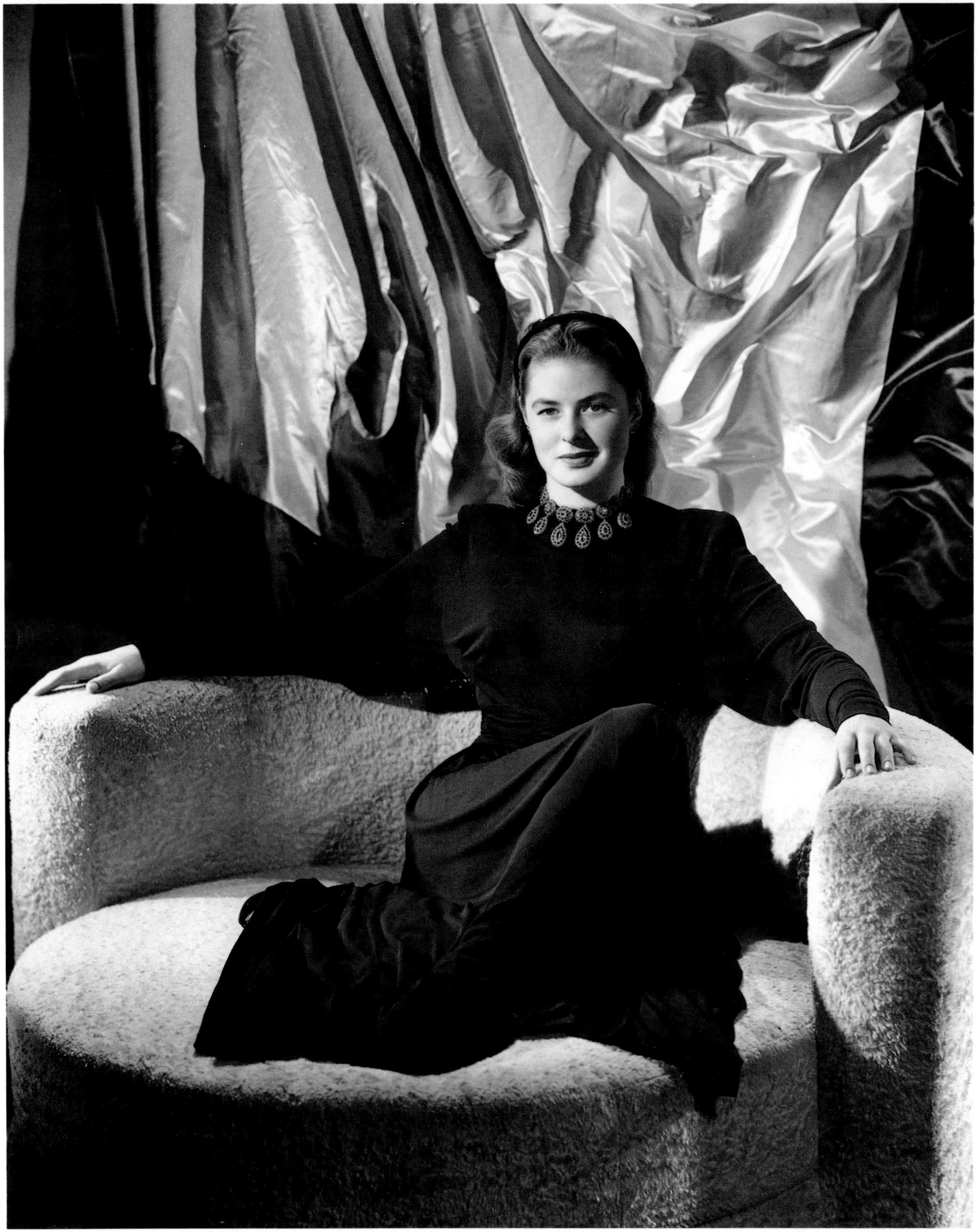

61

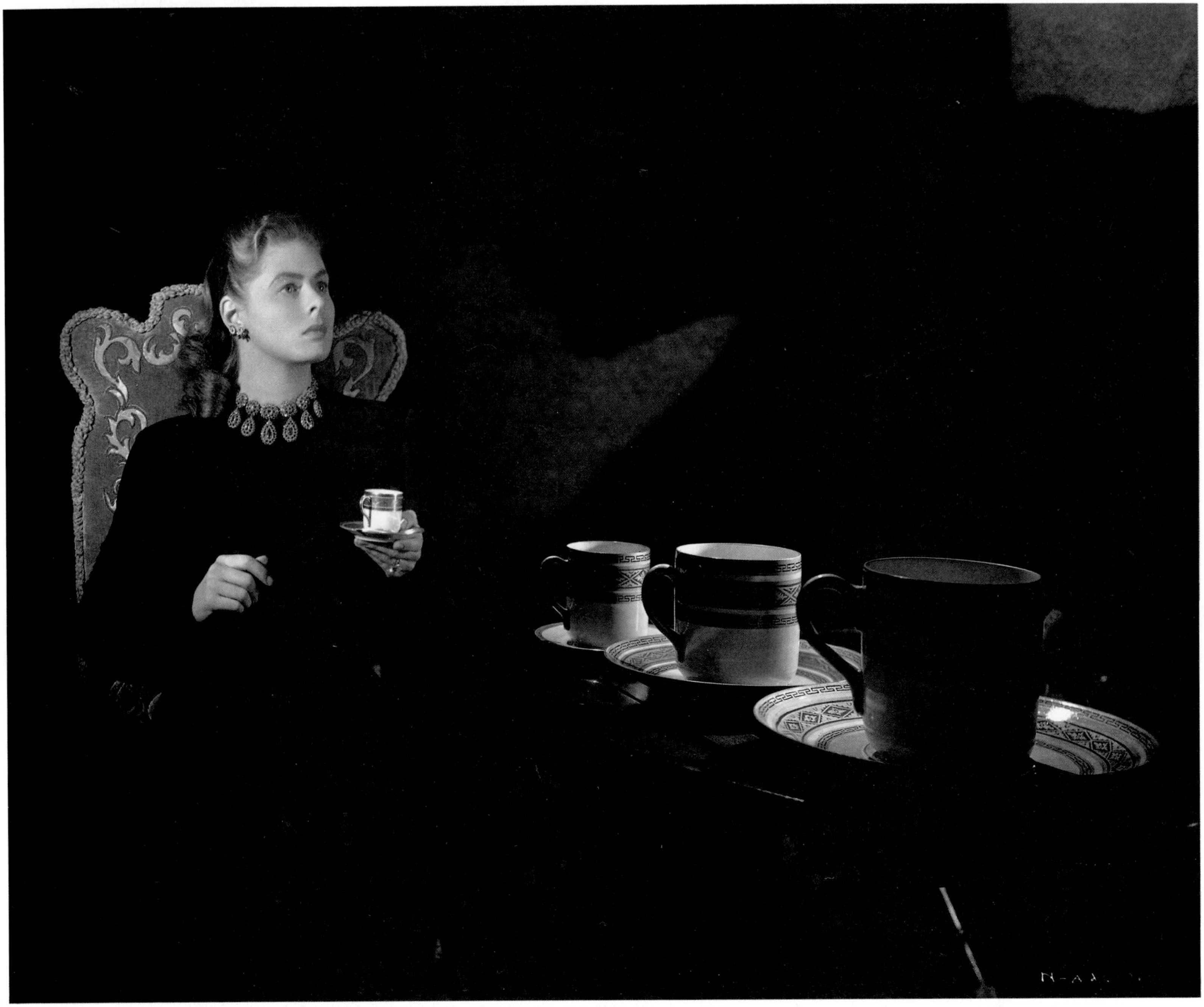

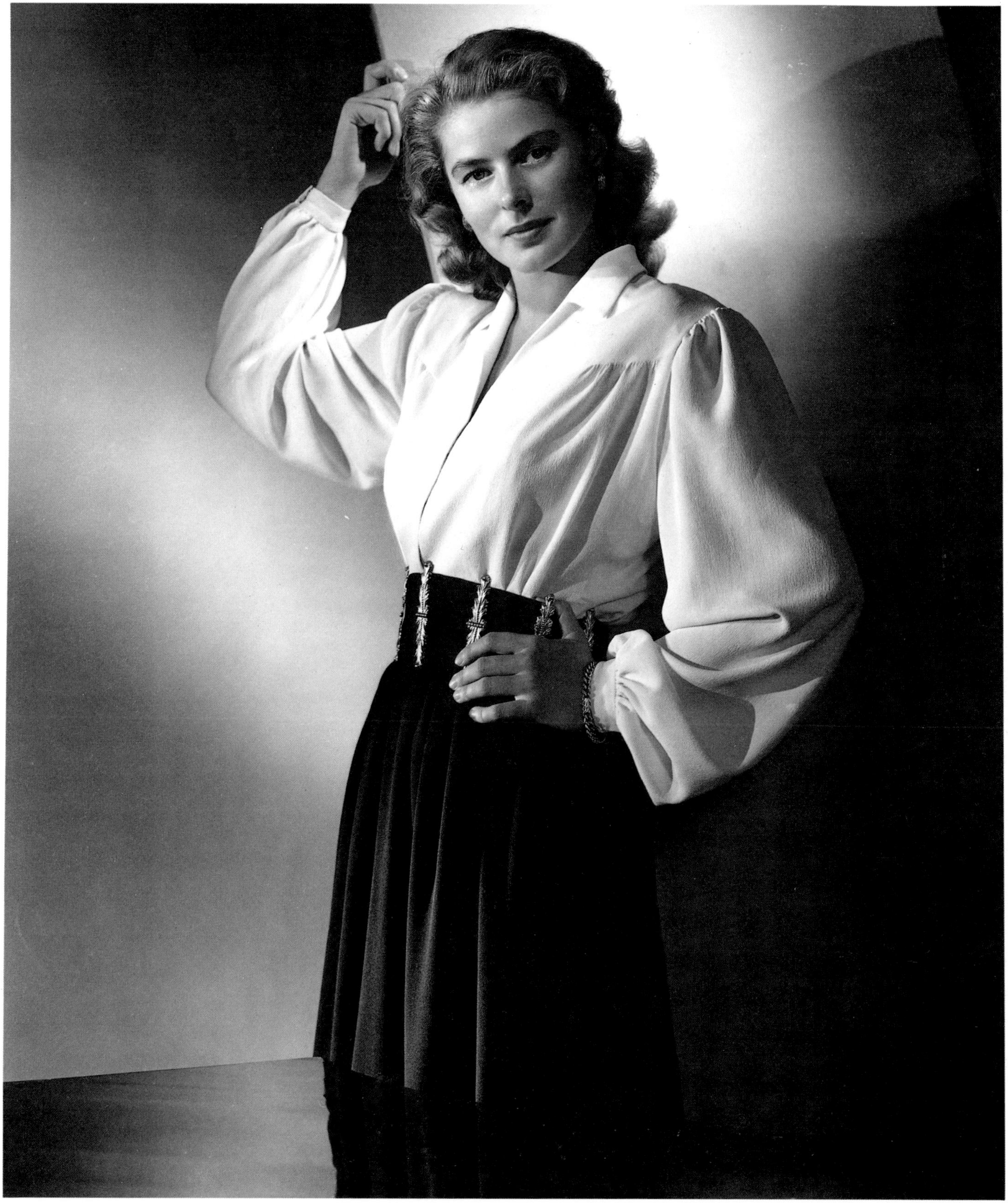

64

65

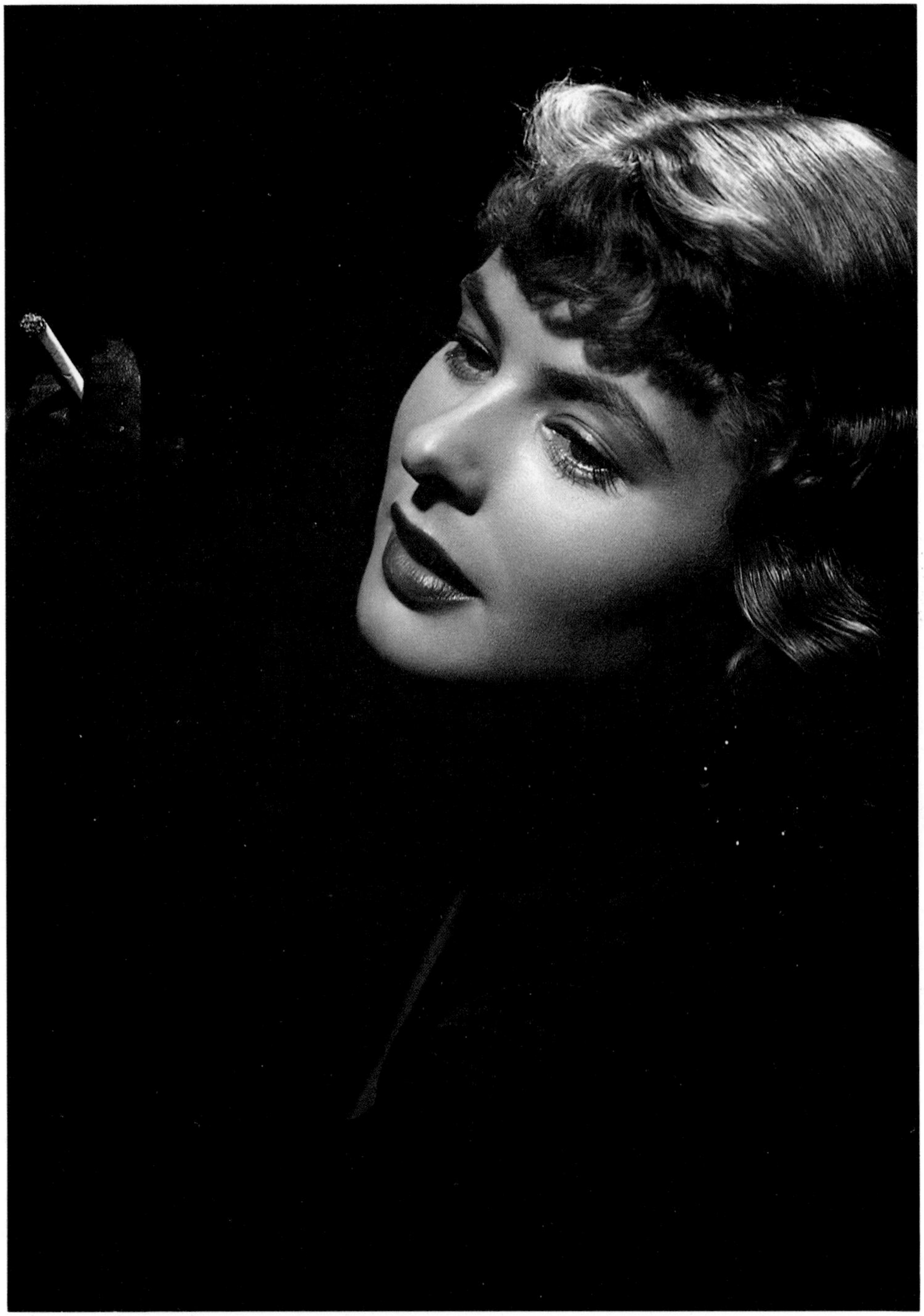

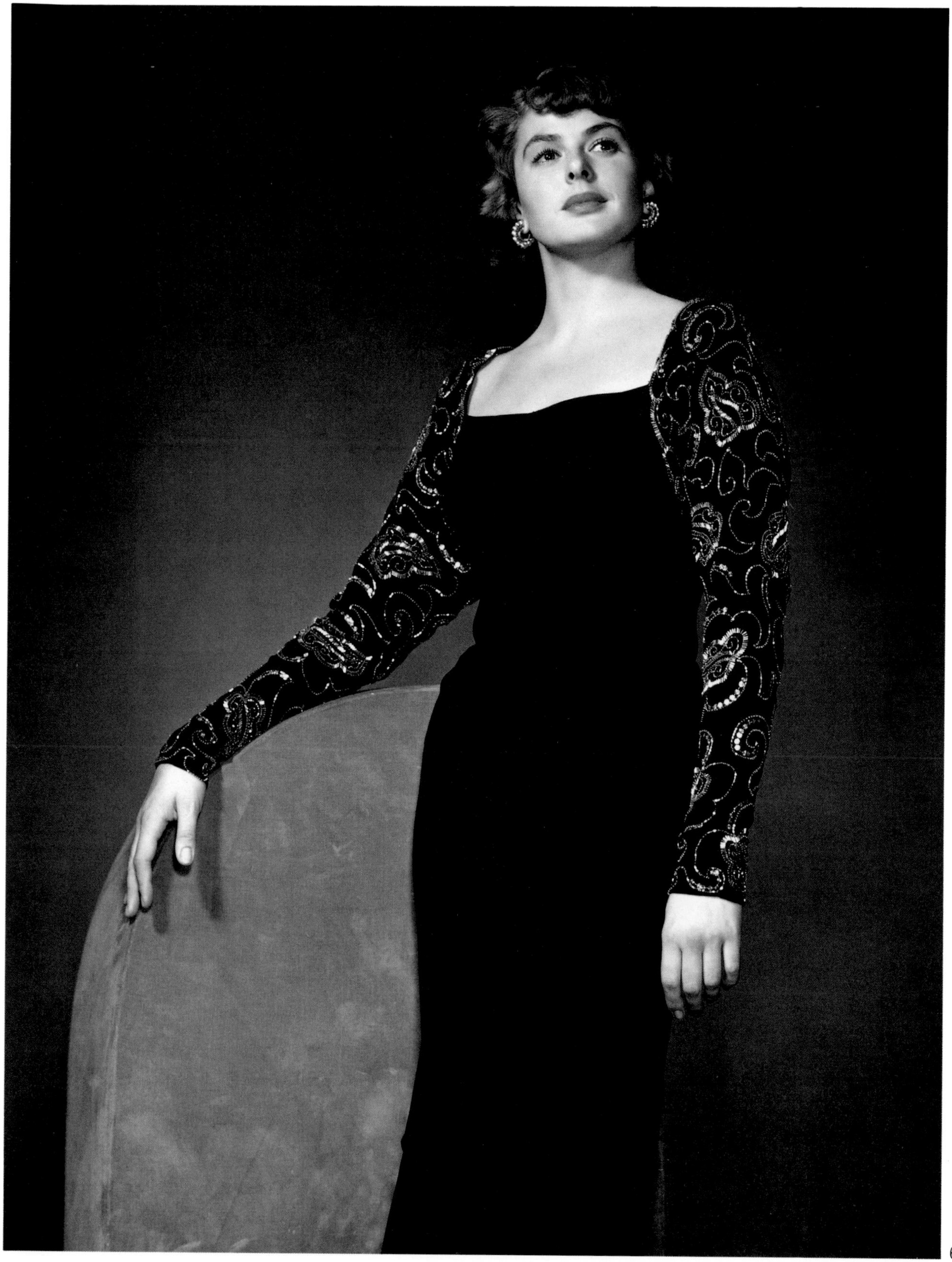

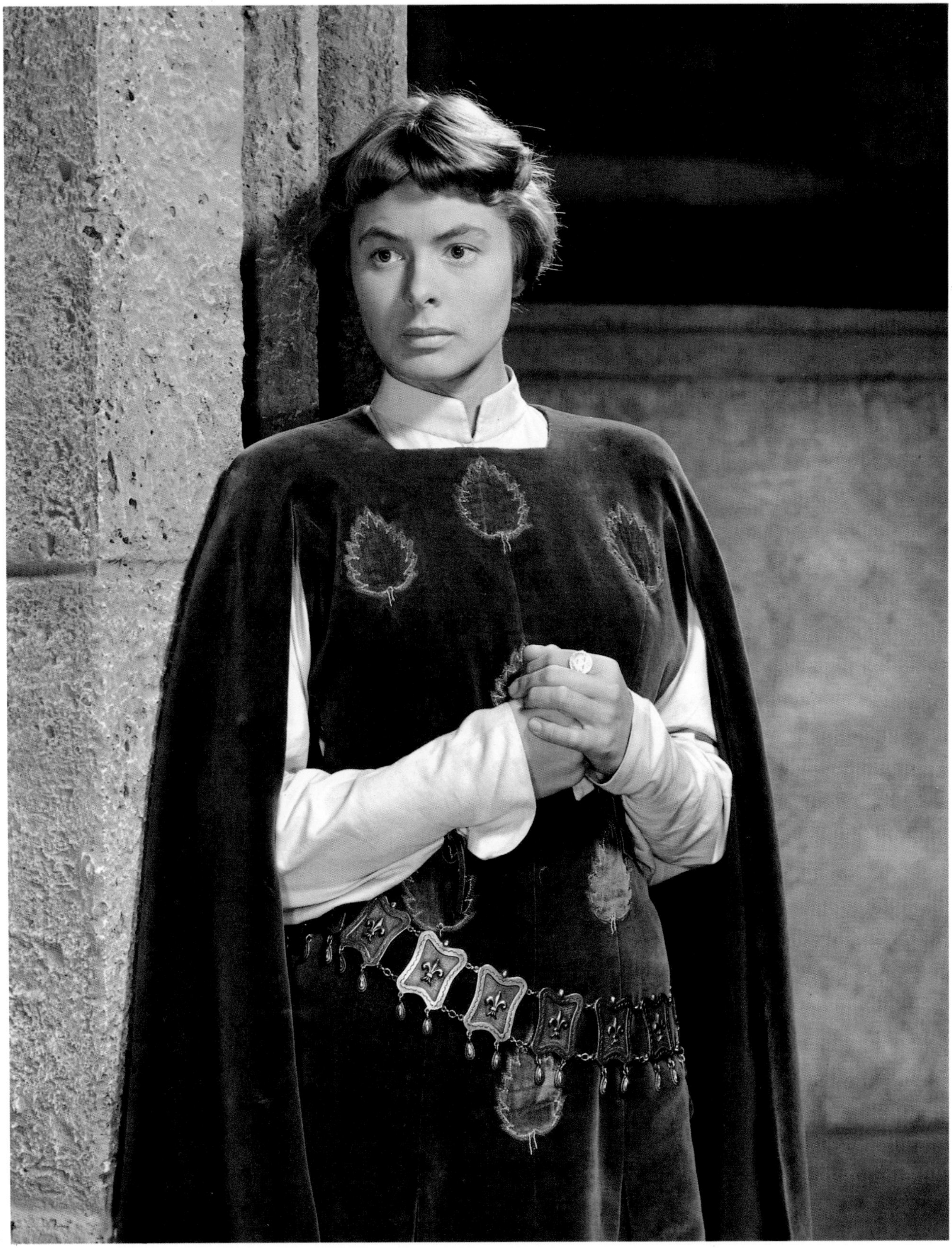

69

Ingrid Bergman

71

72

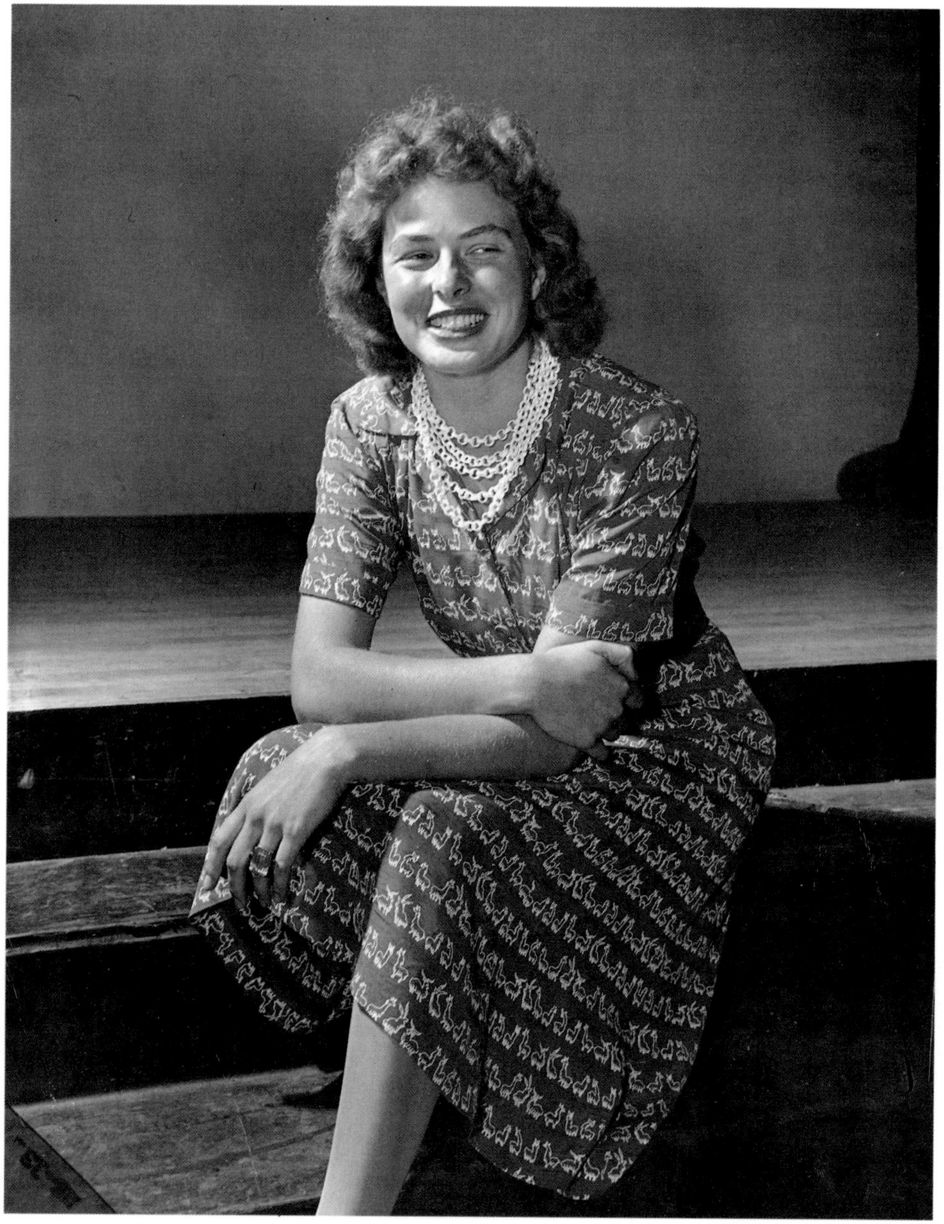

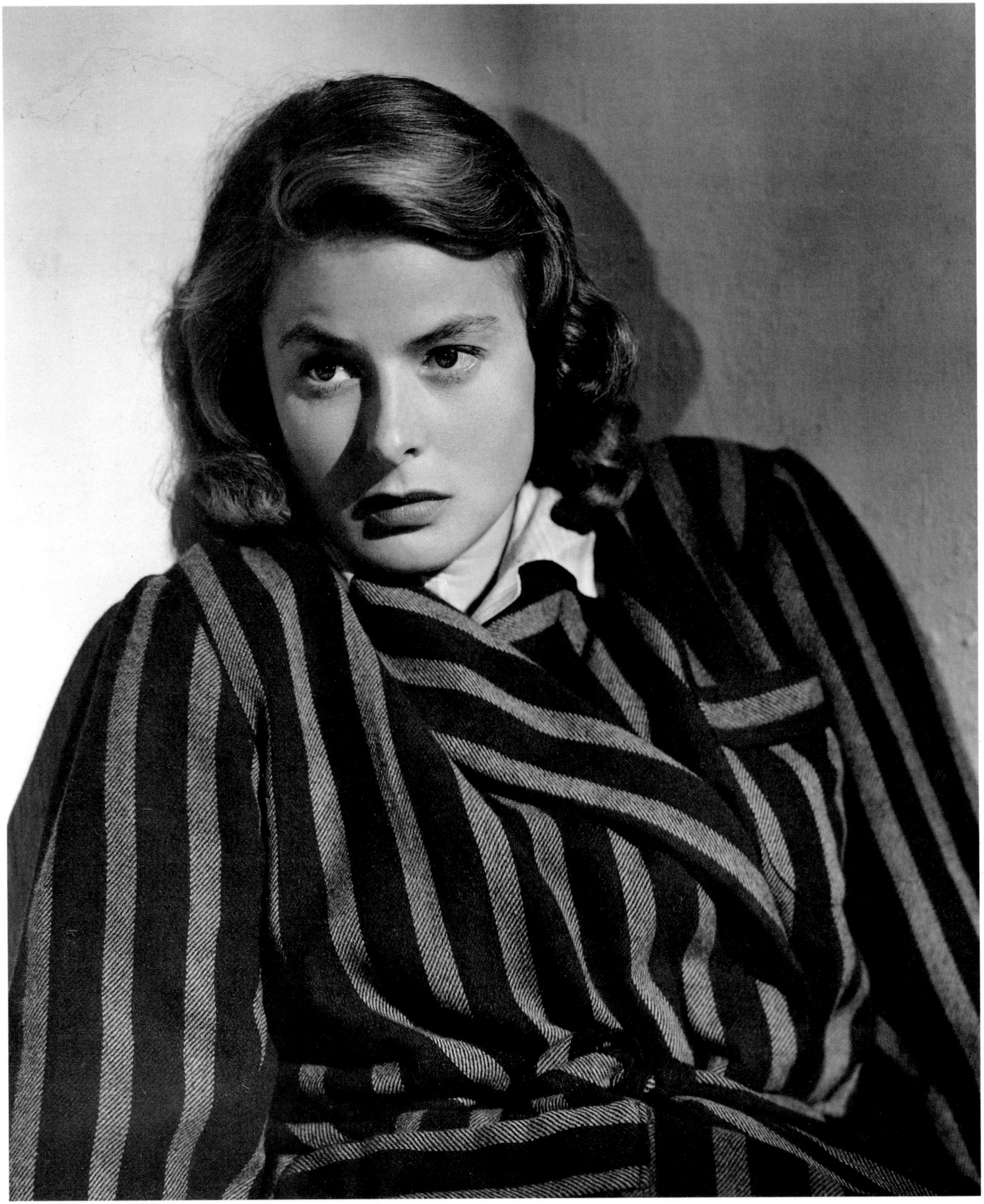

75

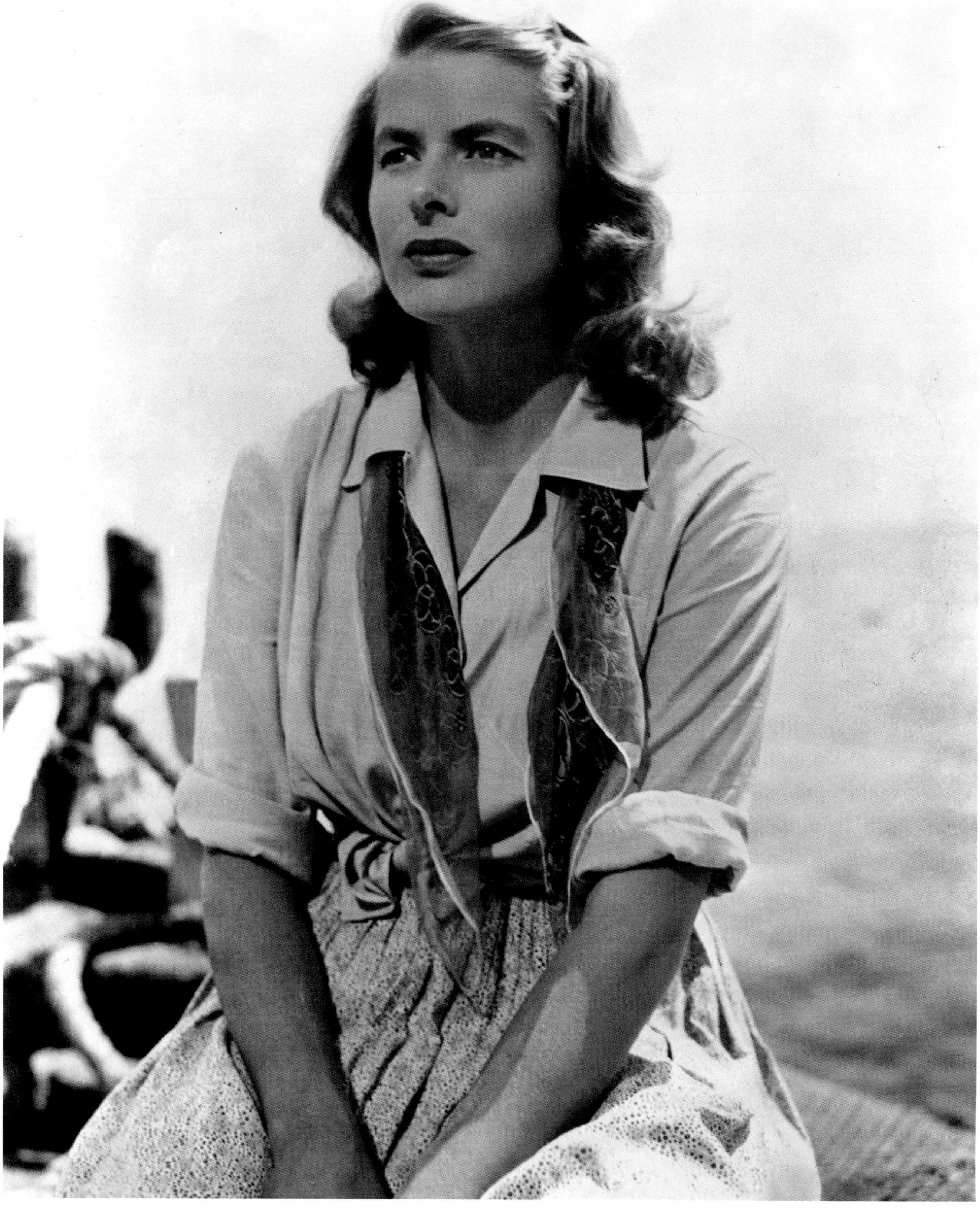

77

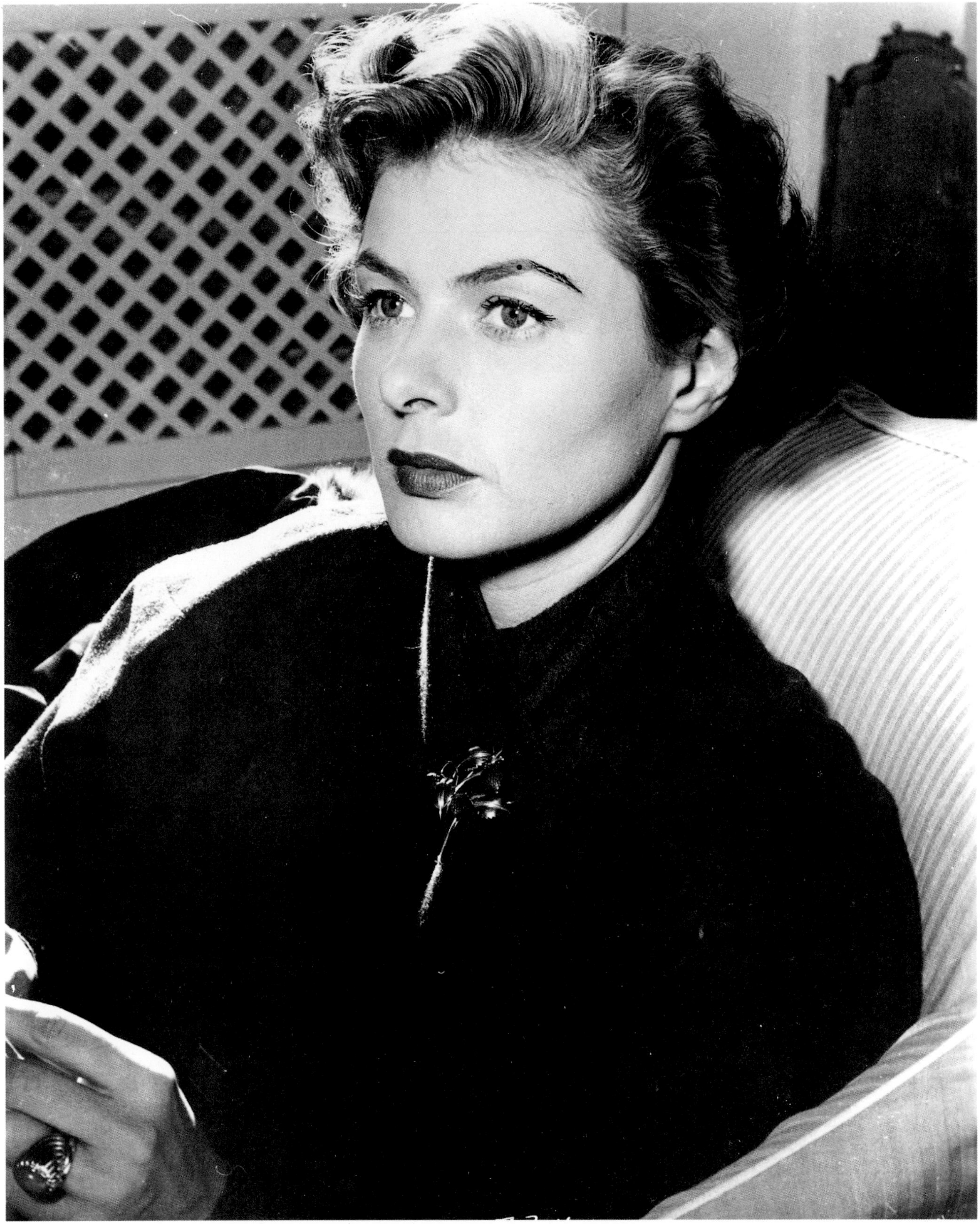

79

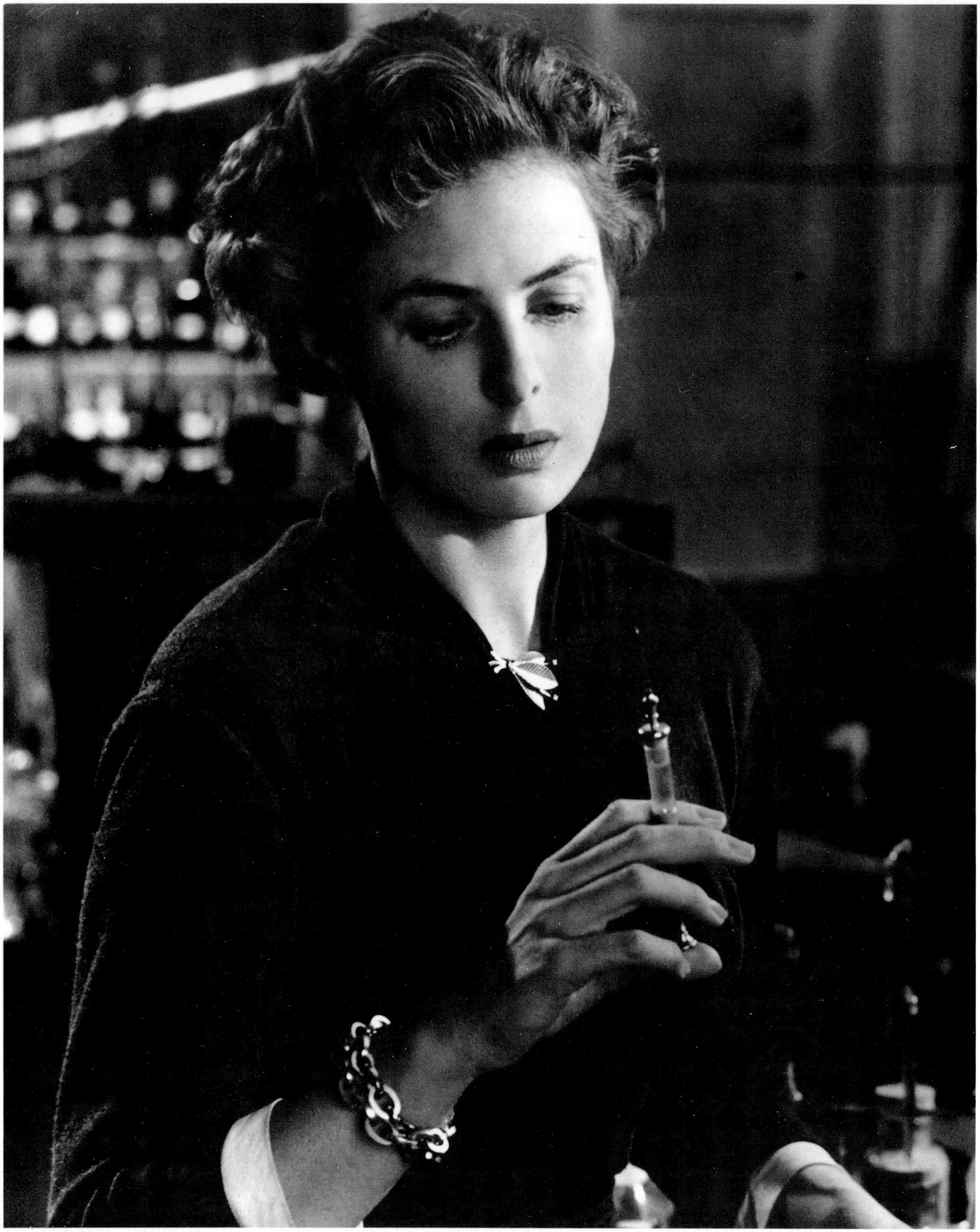

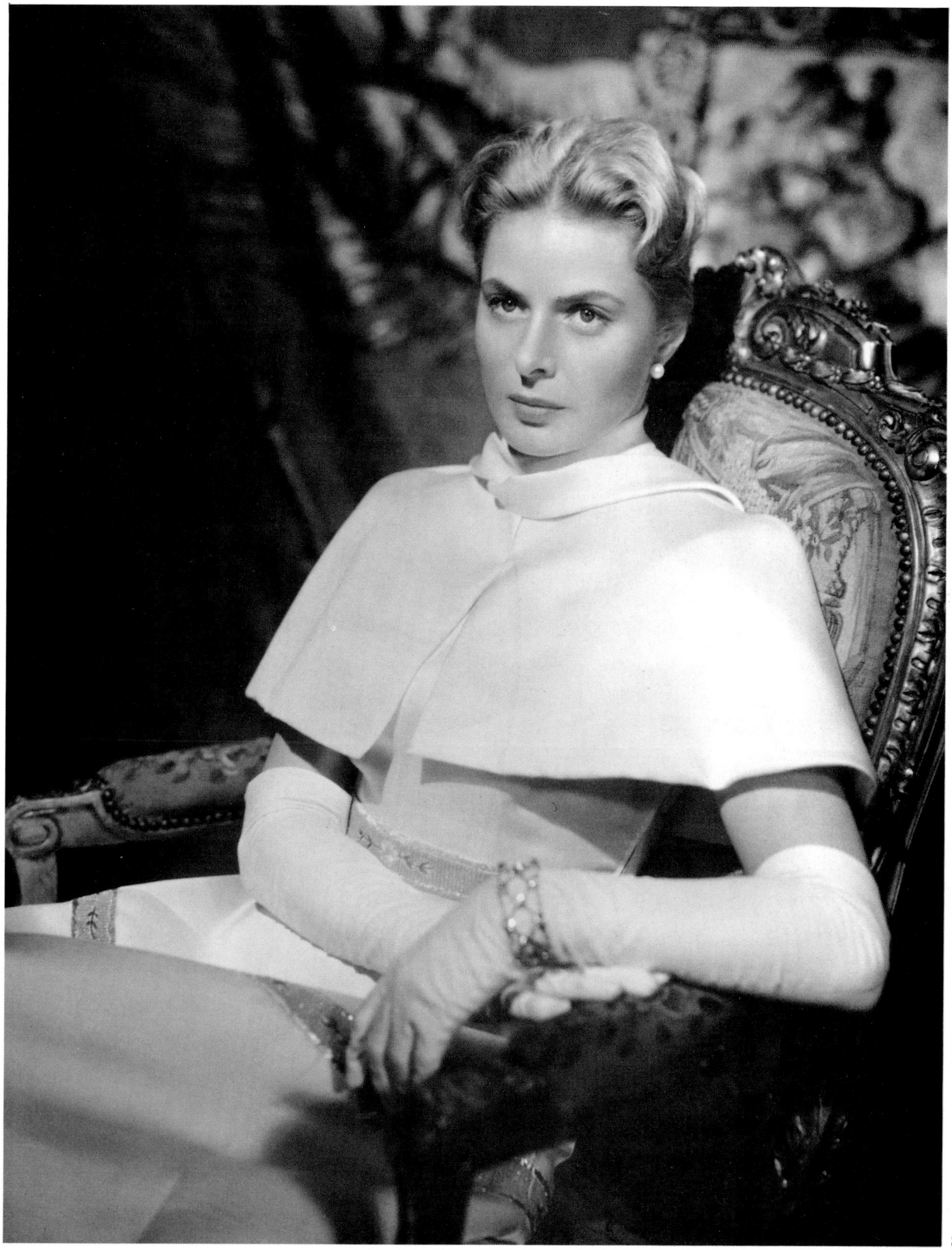

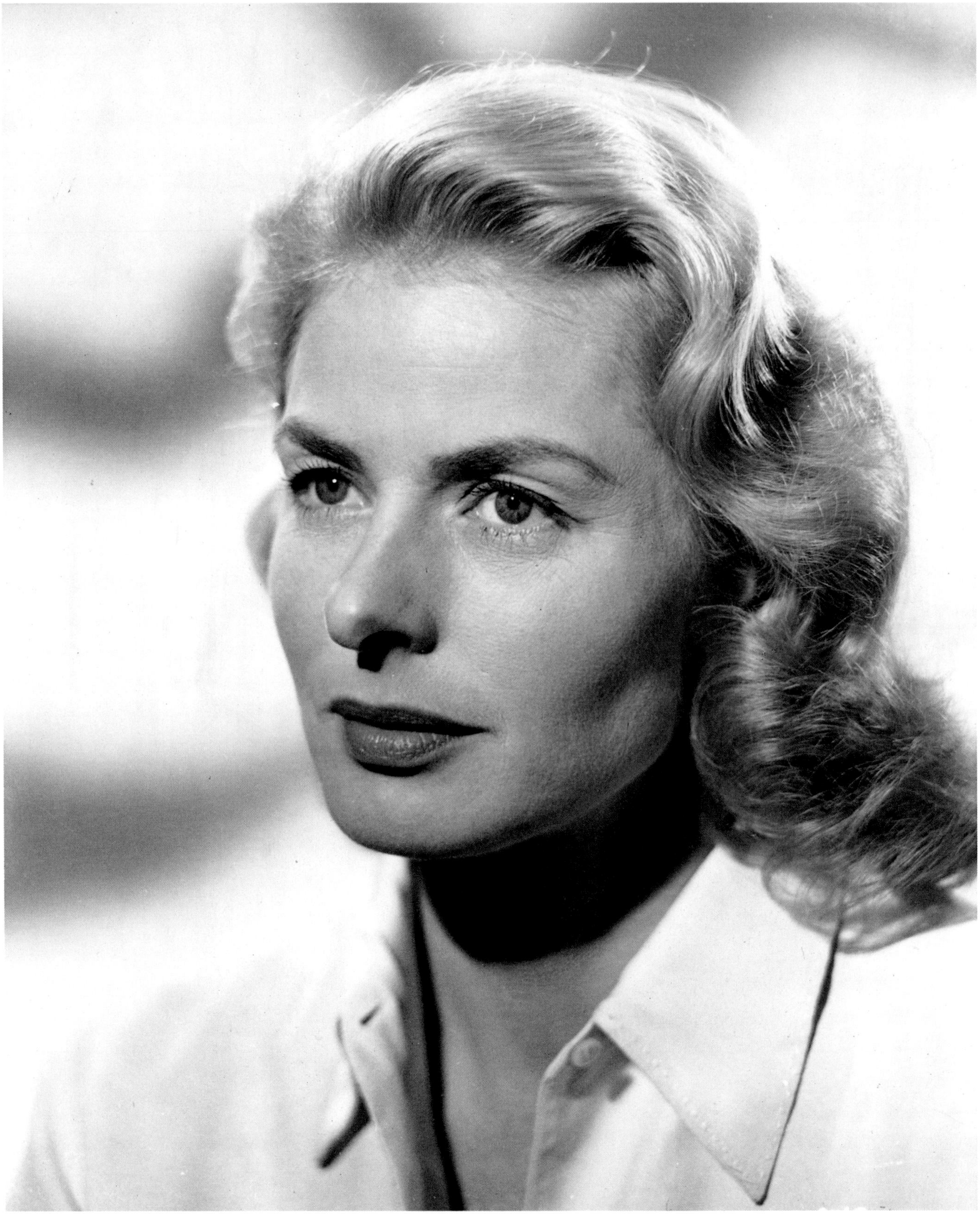

83

84

85

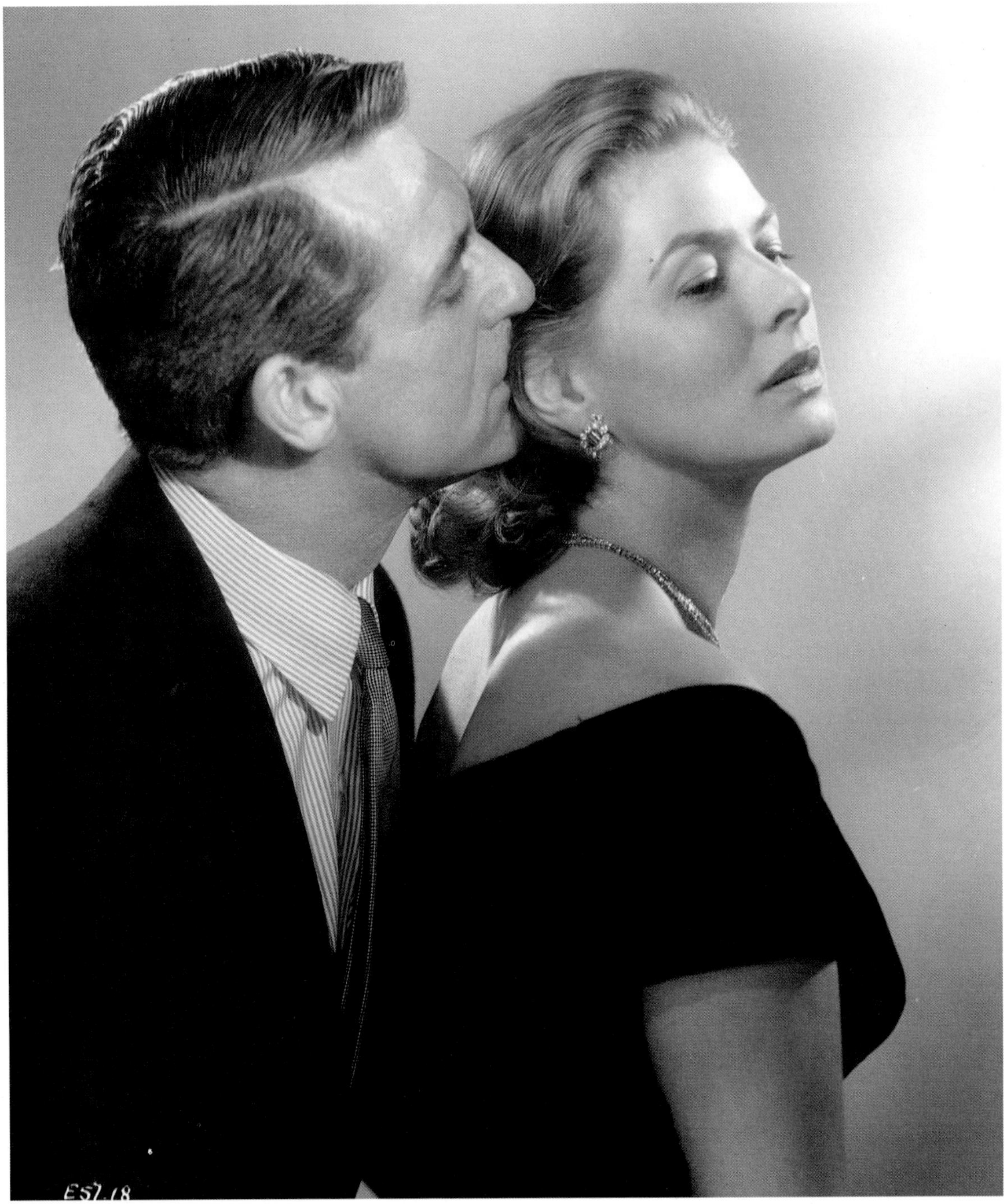
E57.18

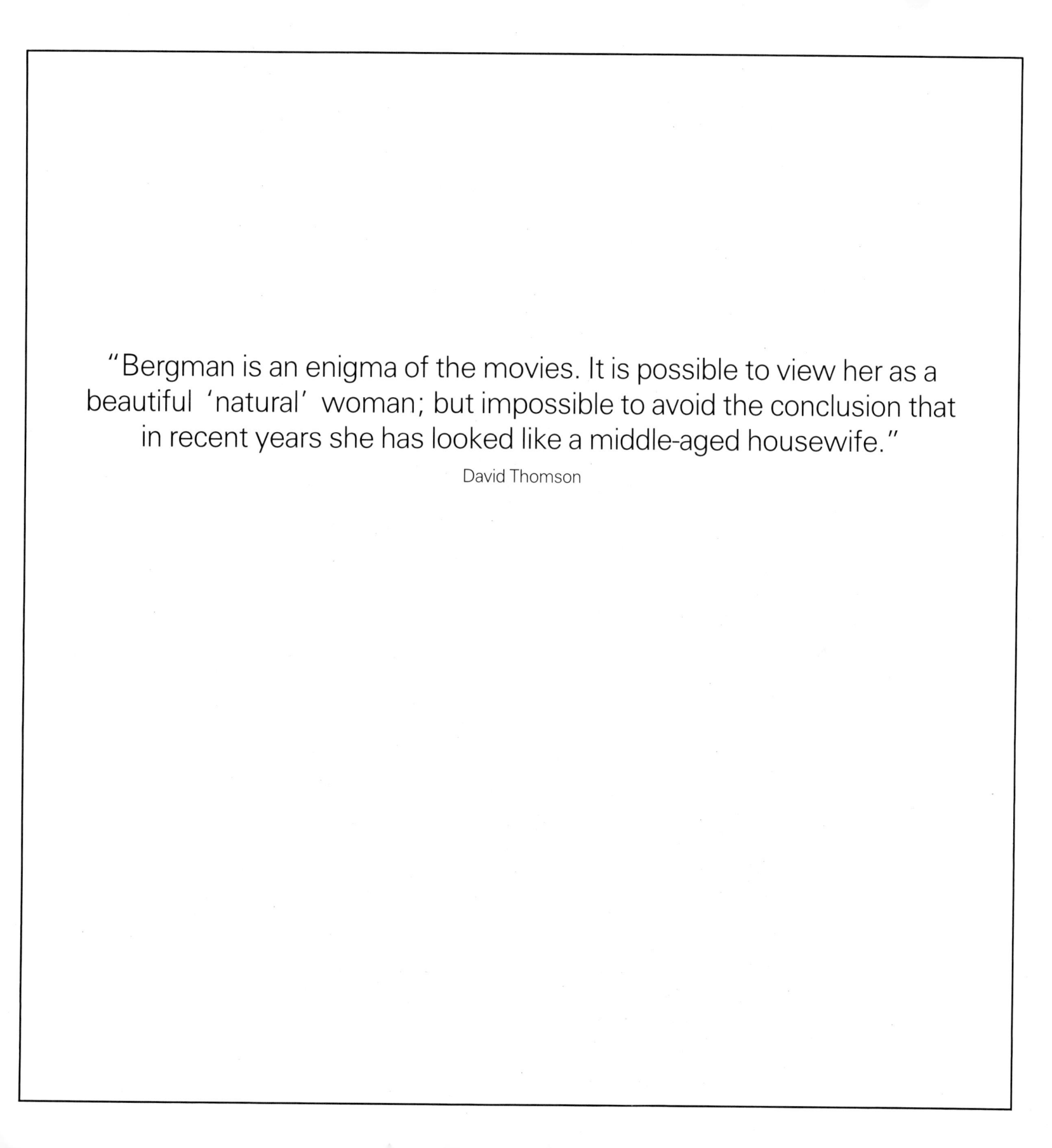

"Bergman is an enigma of the movies. It is possible to view her as a beautiful 'natural' woman; but impossible to avoid the conclusion that in recent years she has looked like a middle-aged housewife."

David Thomson

"With her performance in The Inn of the Sixth Happiness
Ingrid Bergman shows herself to be the greatest film actress now
working anywhere in the world.
She is also, I think, the screen's most beautiful woman.
That serene smile, and those great eyes
give her a radiance for which anyone tired of the
manufactured sex symbols can be most grateful."

Anthony Carthew, Daily Herald

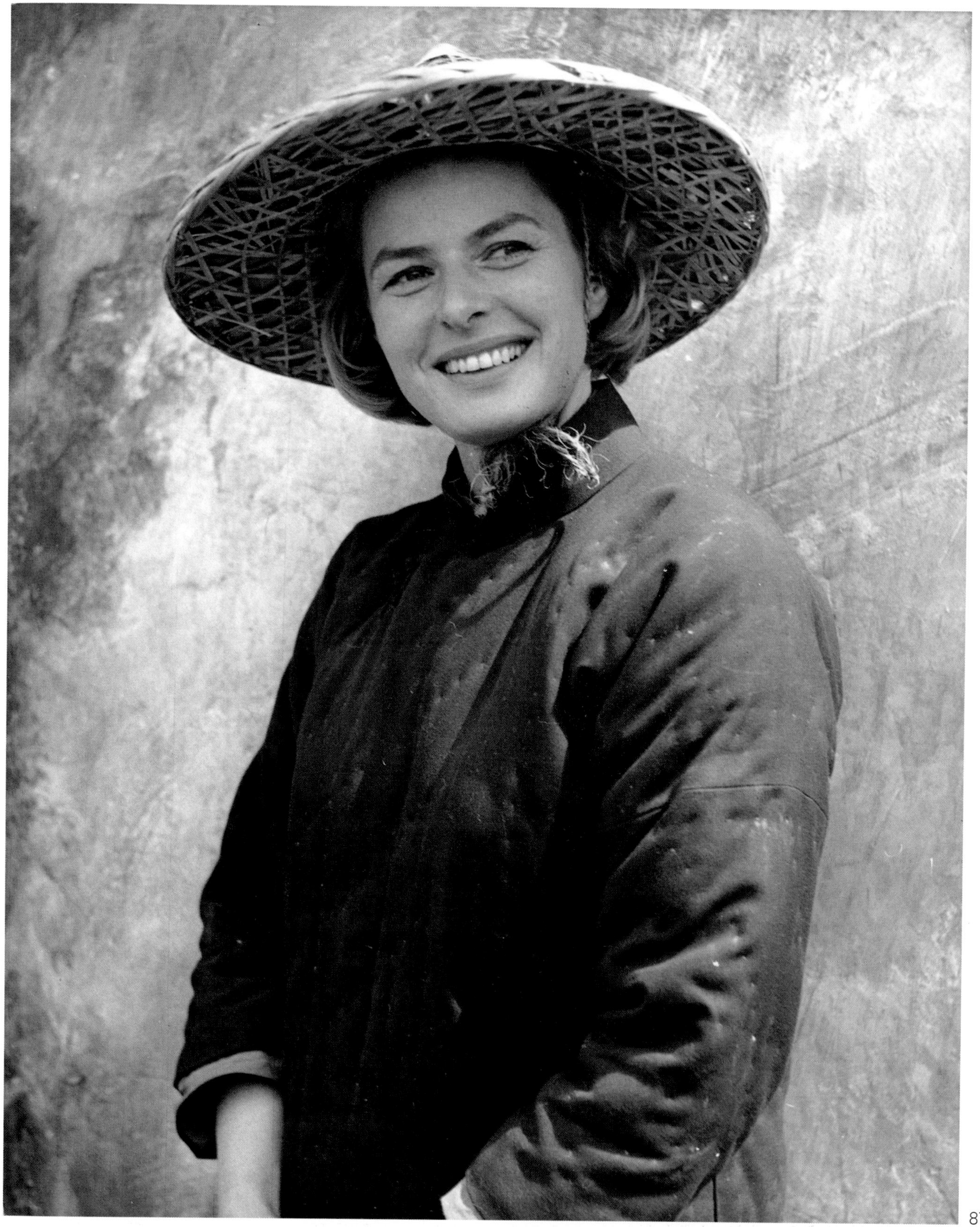

88

89

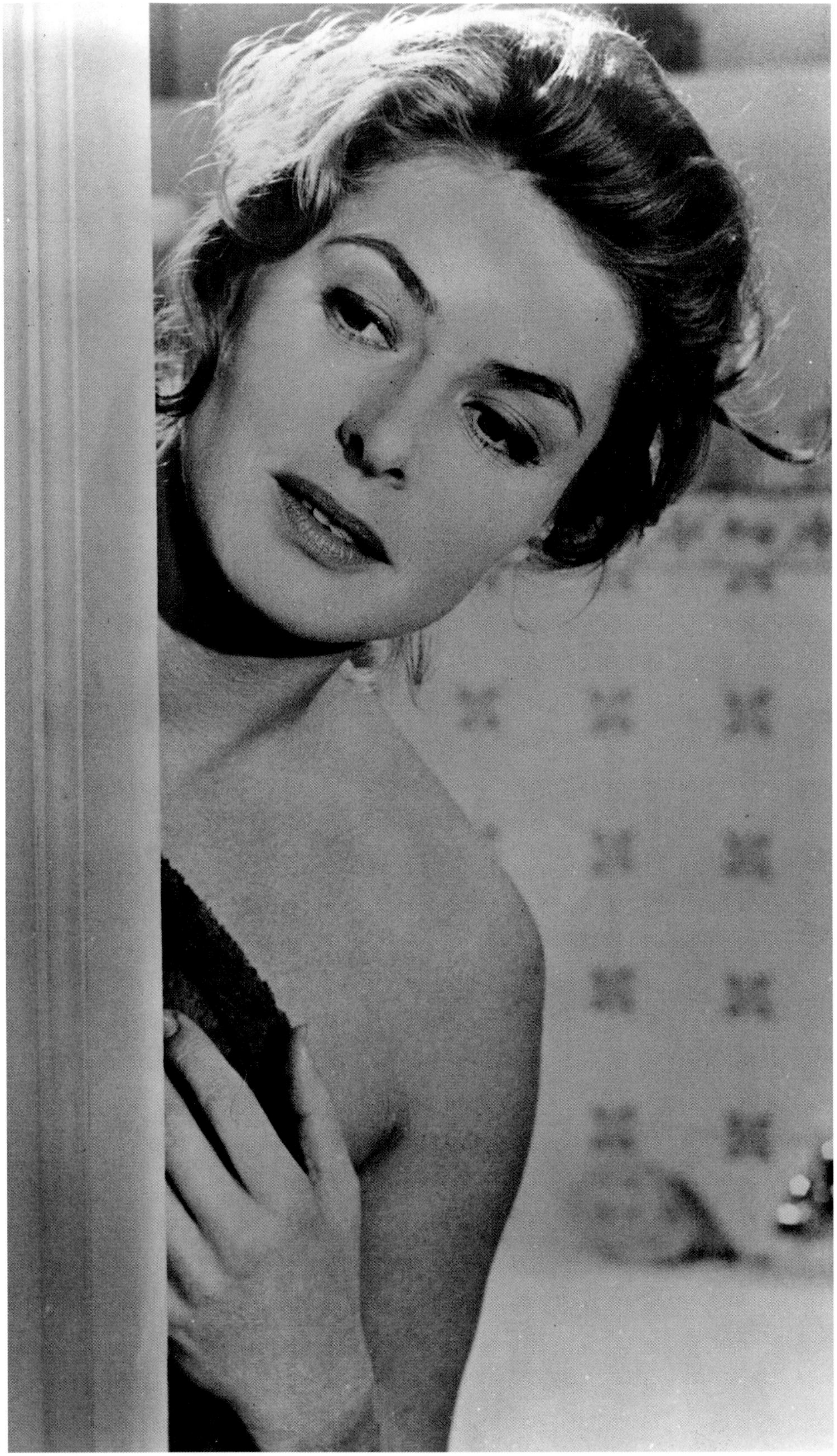

91

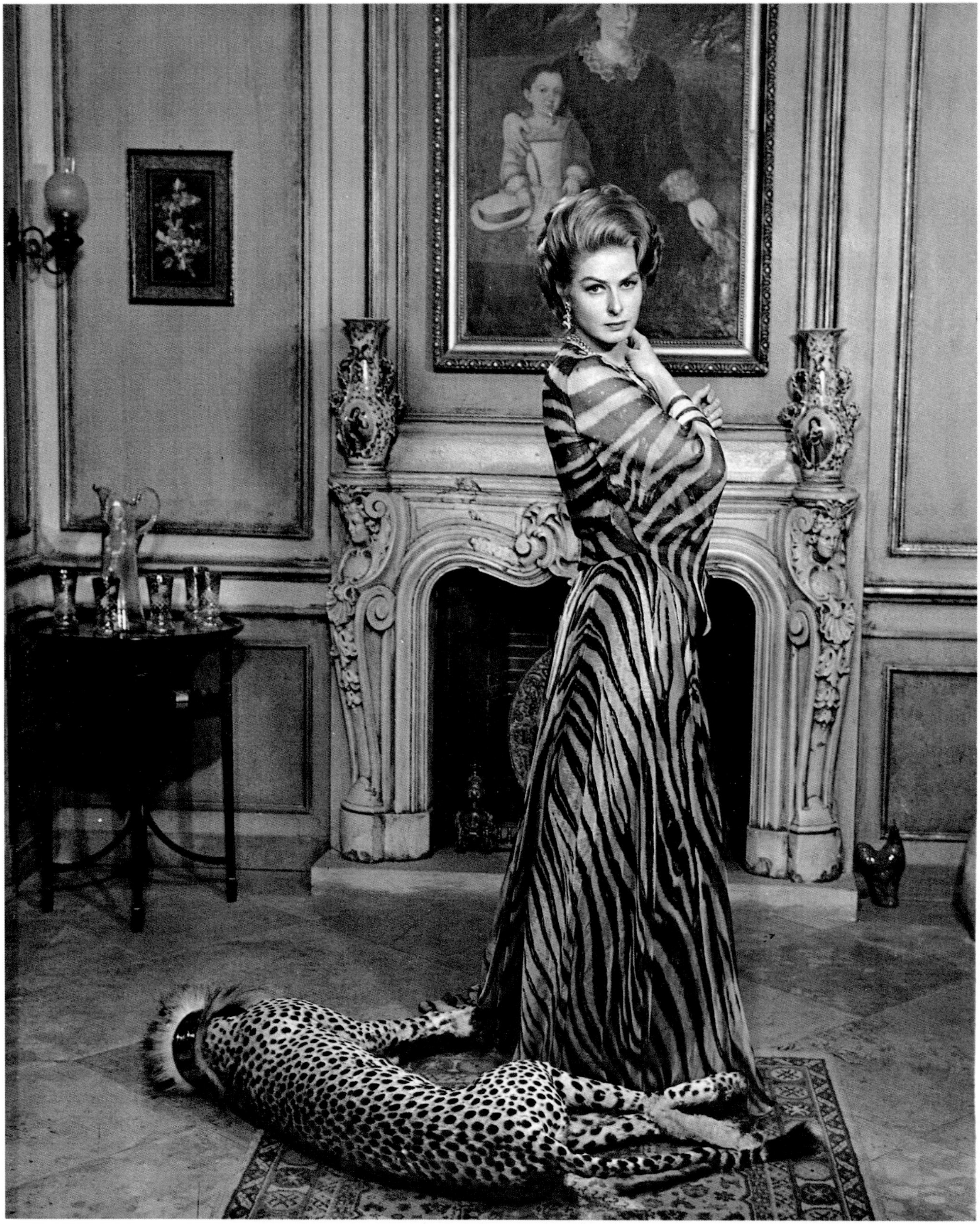

"I note that Bergman is 69½ inches tall.
Is it possible she is actually this high?"

David O. Selznick

93

94

95

96

97

PHOTOGRAPHY, FILM STARS AND ART

At some point in his life everybody has been photographed – celebrities more than most, film stars more than any. A singer projects his personality through music; an actor through his voice; a writer by way of his pen; a model through stance, and so on. But the movie star is the one who, as the primary condition of his profession, projects through appearance. It is his look, his face, that is his fortune. Not mere surface beauty, but the skill, gift, a culpable innocence he has managed to retain, that allows his face to become a mirror to thoughts, continuous and shifting, not just to impersonate feeling but to become that feeling, to reveal the primitive forces of emotion whether fearsome, awesome, ugly or glorious, as spellbinding because shared. As varied as filmstars are in type they reach across all borders to link cultures through the emotions shared by everyone. That is one aspect, and perhaps the most important, of what is meant by the charisma of the film star, his ability to embody the potential of spectators' lives – the missing drama, the lost chance, lived out, up there, on film, by the surrogate and ideal self, with all the enhancements of close-ups, dissolves and an appropriate musical score to make the illusion complete.

'Let us . . . on your imaginary forces work', Shakespeare's chorus implores his audience at the start of *Henry V*. 'Think, when we talk of horses, that you see them.' The film star, the personality specifically born out of, shaped and designed by the medium, its ideal conveyor, can be that leap of imagination which playwrights before and since Shakespeare have called on their audiences to make. The imaginary forces made flesh; the printed word given life. Gene Tierney *is* Laura, Gary Cooper *is* Longfellow Deeds, Ingrid Bergman *is* Ilsa Lund, and vice versa. They exist in their original form as two separate and unrelated beings: Ingrid Bergman, the actress from Sweden; Ilsa Lund the refugee from Hitler's Europe on her way to America via Casablanca, an author's fiction. The two become one and indivisible when their separate existences are joined on film. Bergman's emotions give life to Ilsa's experiences.

Beauty in a movie star is another expression of the emotion (human, divine?) that inspired the creation of the play, the book, the symphony, the painting. This profession (Art?) has been made possible through the invention of the camera, the discovery of film, the secret life of shadows. See the bright light in the dark? That is the film star.

For a film star to possess or convey this beauty is not contingent on his features matching the conventional standard that dictates perfection – it can be conjured by the camera through lighting, angles and make-up. So-called great natural beauty in and of itself, like that of the former Empress Soraya of Iran, or the British dolly bird, model of the Sixties, Jean Shrimpton, has hardly ever been a sine qua non for screen stardom, though the image we have retained in our memory of the great film stars has been that of powerful beauty. To define this state of conveying emotions and character through beauty, an old word had to be brought out: glamour. Our appreciation of this has to do with the camera, the miracle that is photography. The most extraordinary thing the unforgettable images of film stars tell us about photography is of the camera's ability to reflect the mind, reveal the nerve endings, the thought behind the eyes, the heartbeat. It is art, taken in photography, consummated on film.

Three separate means exist for the creation of art through the camera, one of which is possible in no other medium:

A. Like other artists, the man behind the lens, the photographer, conceives, selects, shapes, creates. The resulting picture is what he wants us to see. He is the artist. He must be a great one to create a picture that is great.

B. The photographer who happens to be in the right place at the right time with his camera, at what Cartier Bresson called 'the decisive moment', need not be much more than a skilled craftsman to be able to produce a single great photograph if what it captures has the ingredients that make it emotionally powerful and timeless: a witness to greatness may be made great as a result. (N.B. Ultimately it is not skill but inspiration that gives a work artistic immortality. But in photography, because of the factor of instantaneousness, a factor that has been built into the camera, photographs possessing their own kind of timeless power can be achieved.) The reason why pictures that might well be considered and accepted seriously as photographic art can be taken by skilled journeymen has to do with the instrument's computer-like ability to integrate and make part of the whole that which is happening before it. Thus, a man who is present with a camera at a moment which turns out subsequently to be of momentous historical or emotional importance (like Dorthea Lange's migrant mother at a moment of total devastation, or, the magnificent newsphoto of St Paul's Cathedral, proud, untouched above the flames of war-bombed London) can be the recorder of history, a participator in the creation of art, a vessel of genius. This sort of photograph tends on the whole to be in the area of news reportage, but this qualification need not make the final object less powerful or profound than, for example, Goya's tortured peasants in *Los Desastres, de la Guerra*, or Picasso's *Guernica*. For while, unlike with Goya and Picasso, the talent to conceive or create a dramatic work of that force may be absent in the photographer, the impact in such a work is inherent in the situation and the camera has captured it. Of course the photographer was present, and may have had the wit to frame or compose the event for maximum impact, but framing is often done later on, in the dark-room. Moreover, the same image would have been captured if an automatic camera could have been set up and programmed to take a photograph every second. If it could do this for a long enough period in a place where some momentous effect might have been anticipated, a similar photograph to the one which the photographer took would have been taken by the unmanned camera. In recent years, action and news photographers who used to work for the weekly photo magazines like *Life*, *Look*, *Picture Post*, *Stern* and *Paris Match* are honoured by exhibitions in major museums around the world for just this sort of photograph. War is a great arena for conferring artistic greatness on men who might more appropriately be called historians writing with the lens than photographers creating art out of the human condition. This proves perhaps that, with a lapse of time, history can make anything into an art or that news photography can be art just as journalism can be literature. Art without an artist is unique to this medium.

C. Lastly, and most significant for the purpose of this series, there is the art that can result from bringing A and B together, an artist behind the camera, and a co-operative creative subject in front of the camera, two forces in harmony to fuse into a third. This is not the unequal relationship that exists between teacher and pupil or master and apprentice, but even further developed than the tie that exists for example between conductor and composer, for there can never be absolute creative equality there either, whereas in the situation I speak of there is as close to an equal share in the creative relationship as may be humanly possible. Naturally the subject is of paramount importance, needing to retain much of the emotional innocence of childhood while having gained the mental stability to enable him or her it to participate in this creation on a conscious level. The ideal combination is an animal's grace, a child's innocence and a knowledge of what it is to be hungry. After a century of photography and thousands, millions of portraits of all kinds – of wives, husbands, children, bankers, lawyers, poets, painters, politicians – the closest we have got to this is the film star. The film star was made possible because of the camera, and was necessary to reveal photography's hitherto unrecognised emotional power.

Initially photography had captured the popular imagination with its speed, embodying in so many ways the rapid rise of the new post-revolutionary bourgeoisie, as if it had been invented for just this purpose. Working people who had neither the time nor the commitment of the artist to take up painting, and who besides would not have been able to afford portraits painted of them and their loved ones, could afford a photograph and, not long after, with the mass production of cheap cameras, to take their own portraits. PRESTO, just a matter of Hold It, Hold It, Hold It, Hold It, Hold It . . CLICK; and a few days later there would be the results.

Besides this marvel of speed and ease which would make everyone imagine himself a potential photographer, just as the calculator generation overnight felt at ease with higher mathematics, photography initially astonished with its honesty: 'the camera does not lie' was the famous motto. Of course this was just an illusion, a sales gimmick, since it supposed that the camera took pictures by itself and denied the existence of the man behind the camera or that this man might have a point of view. Today, after one and a half centuries of photographs, we not only know that the camera has been made party to countless untruths, but that the miraculous aspect credited to the camera – its creation of images of life-like fidelity – is something which graphic artists can achieve with pen and pencil on paper.

Even so, and perhaps only because of the purely mechanical miracles of the process it has taken photography over a hundred years and a lot of amateur pictures to gain its present recognition as an art form. Today photographs are exhibited in galleries and sold at auctions just like paintings. The sheer overwhelming number of pictures of course served to show up the good ones and thus reassure the critical establishment of the continued validity of the old adage that anything 'good' still takes time, dedication, education and all the other things by which art has been judged and categorized. A cat has four legs, and a dog has four legs, but a cat is not a dog. Thus, everybody could snap a picture, but not everybody was going to be a Steichen; ergo: photography might after all be an art form once standards could be drawn up, and then imposed. Society was re-establishing its dominion over the individual, the supplier over the consumer.

But here again the significant point was being missed. Photography's contribution as an art lay not merely in what people could do with a camera but what they gained *through* the camera. The pleasure to be had from this toy, coupled with the wonder when looking at the results, started to direct a larger share of the people's interest back toward art, removed their feeling of personal unworthiness, their sense of second-class citizenry, and made it possible for them to become joyfully responsive to art as an illumination of their own existence. The photographs they took might be of interest only to themselves and their nearest and dearest, but their guileless fascination with this medium opened their minds and lifted their spirits: if music and art were now almost wholly the preserve of the rich, that was fair enough, as now they had their own art. For at first, with photography ignored as a possible forum for art, there were no teachers to teach them, no guilds to restrict them, no set standards to inhibit them. Instead of being taught, they could learn. Out of that sense of freedom, that enthusiasm, those years of experimentation and continued discovery, photography's subsequent claim to be an art took shape. Unhindered by theory, nobody then realised that photography offered what might be considered an X-ray of man's thoughts, his emotions, his instincts, something which no surgeon's scalpel could ever expose. The camera's gift is to capture and preserve for all time a spark of the human existence in full flame.

When the celebrated Viennese photographer Laszlo Willinger, who had arrived at MGM in 1937 near the end of Hollywood's platinum age of portrait photography, was told to shoot portraits of the beautiful British film star Vivien Leigh fresh from her triumph in *Gone With the Wind*, he felt that, while she reported for the work of providing publicity for her forthcoming film with new portraits, her mind was absent. She looked to him impassive, uninterested, as if she would much rather be elsewhere. She was beautiful but bored. He did not think this would make for a promising sitting. When he looked at the day's shoot, Laszlo, who after ten years in the business should no longer have been surprised, found to his amazement that her face, and especially her eyes, were teeming with a life that he hadn't seen with his naked eye. The camera had not merely recorded her surface appearance but also that interior state he had felt, and which was not of his making. In the portraits and photographs of movie stars, whether pictures taken in galleries or frames from films, we get intimations of a humanity made of immortal imperishable stuffs; as if behind these faces, beneath these skins, are not flesh and bones traced through with veins and arteries, bound up with sinews, enforced with muscle and gristle and fatty tissue, a billion and one red and white corpuscles pulsing – but rather as if they were fleshed out of raw emotion. Emotion tightens the skin of their brows, flares nostrils, raises and lowers cheeks, chins, eyes, rippling across smooth foreheads with pressures as invisible yet powerful as those found when a breeze distorts the surface of a pool invisible to the eye, yet real for all that, as it conducts on the visible features a symphony of pure feeling.

The movie star's nature is to give substance to the things dreams are made of. The great movie stars had this, did this, were this. Gary Cooper's physical beauty, quite special in itself, was ennobled and kept intriguing by the thought behind. It applies to all the pictures and portraits of the great stars. For example, let us consider young Montgomery Clift as George Eastman, a victim in search of his accident in *A Place in the Sun*. Clift's face, in the opening frames of the film, is softened with the sound-track music's questioning yearning, a kind of '*nostalgie de la mort*', and his right to have a dream is represented by the sun-tanned girl painted across the highway billboard. Without the billboard, the music, the signs and sounds that lend clarity to his expression, the portrait taken of him in that moment with the large dark, thirsty eyes, lean patched cheeks sunk even further in dreamy reverie, would be recognised as a study of hopelessness, and it would reach out and touch whoever might see it without their knowing why. Later in the film, Clift sees Liz Taylor for the first time – eighteen, dressed in white, blue-black hair, liquid eyes, radiant with her own youth and the privilege conferred by wealth, a girl in a room full of friends and admirers, impervious to the unguarded stare of a stranger whose expression is the sum of yearning. The nakedness of his feelings, his desire, his ambition and hunger for this girl, and the other emotions he experiences as he goes through this film to his destiny with the hangman, are all hauntingly beautiful images.

Each of the books in this series is devoted to a screen Legend – which, for want of a better word, helps to define those who, like Montgomery Clift, had this remarkable ability more highly developed than others who might have been starred in films but never achieved this degree of audience rapport. The series is intended to show this photographic phenomenon even as it celebrates the great movie stars in photos selected, one hopes, to please the fan, the connoisseur and the lover of good photography. Here are the stars who were loved more devotedly, more intensely, and whose appeal outlasted their own generation and even those generations that came after. Their looks triggered emotions, and something more. In collaboration with the masters of Hollywood studio portrait photography they produced the unforgettable portraits of this century. In this gallery of photos, consisting not only of studio portraits but also of publicity shots, private snaps, off-set photos, news pictures etc., we can if we wish trace the evolution of personalities like Rudolph Valentino and see what made him the silent era's 'great lover'; stars like Joan Crawford, Clark Gable and Gary Cooper, whose careers were made possible through photography and would probably not have existed without; and others who, like Ingrid Bergman or Bette Davis, Henry Fonda, Humphrey Bogart or James Stewart, had careers that touched on several branches of show-business but still found their fullest realisation and success on the screen. And perhaps, too, we can observe some of this wonder that makes photography unique as an art.

JOHN KOBAL

THE PHOTOGRAPHS

Cover: photograph by Laszlo Willinger 1941, MGM
Frontispiece: *Indiscreet* 1958, studio portrait, Warner Brothers

1. *Intermezzo* 1936, Svenskfilmindustri
2. *The Yellow Rolls-Royce* 1965, MGM
3. *Swedenheilms* 1935, Svenskfilmindustri
4. *En Kvinnas Ansikte* 1938, Svenskfilmindustri
5. Studio portrait 1941, MGM
6. *Spellbound* 1945, photograph by Madison Lacy, Selznick International
7. *Europa '51* 1951, IFE
8. photograph by Ernest Bachrach 1946, RKO
9. Branningar 1935, Svenskfilmindustri
10. *Pa Solsidan* 1936, with Edvin Adolphson, Svenskfilmindustri
11. *Pa Solsidan* 1936, Svenskfilmindustri
12. *Pa Solsidan* 1936, Svenskfilmindustri
13. *Intermezzo* 1936, with Gosta Ekman, Svenskfilmindustri
14. *Dollar* 1938, Svenskfilmindustri
15. i*Dollar* 1938, Svenskfilmindustri
16. *Dollar* 1938, Svenskfilmindustri
17. *En Kvinnas Ansikete* 1938, Svenskfilmindustri
18. *En Enda Natt* 1939, Svenskfilmindustri
19. *En Enda Natt* 1939, Svenskfilmindustri
20. *Die Vier Gessellen* 1938, UFA
21. *Intermezzo* 1939, with Leslie Howard, Selznick International
22. Photograph by Bob Coburn 1939, Selznick International
23. *Intermezzo* 1939, photograph by Charles E. Kerlee
24. *Intermezzo* 1939, photograph by Charles E. Kerlee
25. *Juninatten* 1940, Svenskfilmindustri
26. Photograph by A. L. 'Whitey' Schaefer 1941, Columbia Pictures
27. Photograph by John Engstead 1939, Selznick International
28. Photograph by John Engstead 1939, Selznick International
29. Photograph by A. L. 'Whitey' Schaefer 1941, Columbia Pictures
30. Photograph by A. L. 'Whitey' Schaefer 1941, Columbia Pictures
31. Photograph by Laszlo Willinger 1941, MGM
32. 1941, Selznick International
33. Photograph by Laszlo Willinger 1941, MGM
34. *Rage in Heaven* 1941, MGM
35. *Dr Jekyll and Mr Hyde* 1941, MGM
36. *Casablanca* 1942, with Humphrey Bogart, Warner Brothers
37. Photograph by Scotty Welbourne, 1942, Warner Brothers
38. 1943, Warner Brothers
39. Photograph by Scotty Welbourne 1942, Warner Brothers
40. Studio portrait 1943, RKO
41. Studio portrait 1943, RKO
42. *For Whom the Bell Tolls 1943*, on set, *Paramount*
43. Photograph by A. L. 'Whitey' Schaefer 1943, Paramount
44. *Gaslight* 1944, MGM
45. *Gaslight* 1944, MGM
46. With Gary Cooper 1944
47. *Spellbound* 1945, photograph by Madison Lacy, Selznick International
48. *The Bells of St Mary's* 1945, RKO
49. *Spellbound* 1945, photograph by Madison Lacy, Selznick International
50. *Spellbound* 1945, off set, Selznick International
51. Studio portrait 1945, RKO
52. Photograph by Ernest Bachrach 1945, RKO
53. Photograph by John Engstead 1945, RKO
54. *Saratoga Trunk* 1945, photography by Scotty Welbourne, Warner Brothers
55. *Saratoga Trunk* 1945, photograph by Jack Woods, Warner Brothers
56. *Saratoga Trunk* 1945, photograph by Scotty Welbourne, Warner Brothers
57. *Saratoga Trunk* 1945, with Gary Cooper, Warner Brothers
58. Photograph by Ernest Bachrach 1946, RKO
59. *Notorious* 1946, with Cary Grant, Photograph by Ernest Bachrach, RKO
60. *Notorious* 1946, studio portrait by Ernest Bachrach, RKO
61. *Notorious* 1946, studio portrait by Ernest Bachrach, RKO
62. *Notorious* 1946, studio portrait by Gaston Longet
63. Photograph by Ernest Bachrach 1946, RKO
64. *Arch of Triumph* 1948, photograph by Madison Lacy, Enterprize-United Artists
65. *Arch of Triumph* 1948, with Charles Boyer, Enterprize-United Artists
66. *Arch of Triumph* 1948, Enterprize-United Artists
67. Studio portrait 1948, RKO
68. *Joan of Arc* 1948, photograph by Carlyle Blackwell Jnr, RKO
69. Joan of Arc 1948, RKO
70. *Under Capricorn* 1949, Warner Brothers
71. *Under Capricorn* 1949, Warner Brothers
72. Studio portrait 1949, Warner Brothers
73. Photograph by Morris Engel 1947
74. *Stromboli* 1950, RKO
75. *Stromboli* 1950, RKO
76. *Stromboli* 1950, RKO
77. *Europa '51* 1951, IFE Releasing Corps
78. *Journey to Italy* 1954, Titanus
79. Studio portrait 1954
80. *Fear* 1955, Minerva Films
81. *Anastasia* 1956, Twentieth Century Fox
82. Studio portrait 1956, Twentieth Century Fox
83. Elena et Les Hommes (Paris Does Strange Things) 1957, Warner Brothers
84. Studio portrait 1957, Warner Brothers
85. Studio portrait 1958, Warner Brothers
86. *Indiscreet* 1958, with Cary Grant, Warner Brothers
87. *The Inn of the Sixth Happiness* 1958, Twentieth Century Fox
88. *The Inn of the Sixth Happiness* 1958, Twentieth Century Fox
89. *Goodbye Again* 1961, United Artists
90. *Goodbye Again* 1961, United Artists
91. *Goodbye Again* 1961, with Anthony Perkins, United Artists
92. *The Visit* 1964, Twentieth Century Fox
93. *The Visit* 1964, with Anthony Quinn, Twentieth Century Fox
94. *The Yellow Rolls-Royce* 1965, studio portrait, MGM
95. *Cactus Flower* 1969, studio portrait, Columbia
96. *Walk in the Spring Rain* 1970, Columbia
97. *Walk in the Spring Rain* 1970, Columbia